Garland Studies in Historical Demography

Stuart Bruchey

Allan Nevins Professor Emeritus
American Economic History
Columbia University

GENERAL EDITOR

A Garland Series

At the Crossroads

Fertility of Mexican-American Women

Elizabeth Hervey Stephen

GARLAND PUBLISHING, INC.
New York   London
1989

Library of Congress Cataloging-in-Publication Data

Stephen, Elizabeth H.
At the crossroads : fertility of Mexican American women / Elizabeth Hervey Stephen.
p. cm. — (Garland studies in historical demography)
Includes bibliographical references.
ISBN 0-8240-3397-3 (alk. paper)
1. Fertility, Human—United States. 2. Mexican Americans—Population.
3. Mexican American women. 4. United States—Population.
I. Title. II. Series.
HB915.S74 1989
304.6'32'0896872073—dc20   89-37797

Printed on acid-free 250-year-life paper

Manufactured in the United States of America

To my mother, Bettie

TABLE OF CONTENTS

ACKNOWLEDGEMENTS

This book was made possible first through the support of the University of Texas with a University Fellowship, which allowed me to pursue this research full-time. In addition, the Texas Population Research Center provided computer assistance, and an intellectually stimulating environment in which to conduct the original research. The completion of this book was made possible by the support of Georgetown University and specifically, the Department of Demography.

There are a number of people who deserve special mention. My dissertation committee made invaluable suggestions. I want to thank the committee chairman, Frank Bean, and the members, Omer Galle, Harley Browning, Parker Frisbie, Marvin Eisen, and William Kelly, for all of their help. In addition, I want to express appreciation to the director of computing at the Texas Population Research Center, Thomas Linsley, and his staff who produced the data tapes that were used extensively in this analysis.

At Georgetown University, Beth Soldo, chair of the Department of Demography provided resources for preparation of this book. I thank her in particular for support she has given me throughout my career. Charlie Keely's counsel was extremely helpful, particularly on sections dealing with recent immigration reform issues. Expert typing assistance was provided by Marie Carr, Michelle Zentis, Sharon Heinle, and Lyle Piper.

This book would never have been started if it had not been for the intellectual guidance of Gray Swicegood. His collegiality at all stages of this book have been deeply appreciated.

Georganne O'Connor edited the first version of this book with unending patience. Her friendship has sustained me throughout the writing.

Lastly, I want to thank all of my friends I have not mentioned here by name and all of my family for their support and understanding.

ehs

CHAPTER 1

INTRODUCTION

Immigration to the United States has increased dramatically in the past 30 years, once again approaching levels that occurred around the turn of the century. During the 1960s, 3.3 million legal immigrants entered the country; during the 1970s that number reached 4.5 million persons (U.S. Department of Justice, 1981). The size of the illegal population is unknown, but even conservative estimates indicate that total immigration in the 1970s was at its highest level since 1920 (Massey, 1981). During the 1970s and 1980s, the largest number of immigrants from any one country has been Mexico (U.S. Department of Justice, 1988).

Partly as a result of the increase in absolute numbers of immigrants and specifically illegal aliens, immigration has once again become the object of national policy attention. Because fertility levels have remained low in the United States, immigration represents an increasingly large proportion of the national growth rate (20 percent in 1970). Keely (1972) cites the Interim Report from the Commission on Population Growth and the American Future that stated if immigration continued at 400,000 per year and that if the average family had two children, by the year 2000 there would be 16 million more immigrants and their descendants in the U.S. than were here in 1970. This group of immigrants and their descendants would account for one-fourth of the total population increase during that period. Legislation, such as the Immigration Reform and Control Act of 1986 and its predecessors, the Kennedy and Rodino Bills in the 1970s and the Simpson-Mazzoli Bill in the early 1980s, has been proposed partly in response to public concern over the flow of illegal immigrants into the United States. Numerous articles in the media include concern about the size and differential growth rates of

1

various ethnic/racial groups in the United
States, in addition to economic effects of
recent immigration policy (<u>Business Week</u>, 1983;
Chaze, 1982; McConnell, 1988; Shapiro, 1988;
Thomas, 1983; <u>U.S. News and World Report</u>, 1982).

As a result of increasing levels of
immigration and high fertility rates, the
Mexican origin population is one of the fastest
growing ethnic groups in the United States.
Prior to the 1970s there were few demographic
studies on immigration and fertility in the
Mexican origin population because of a lack of
available data and a general confusion over the
definition of this ethnic group. (See
Hernandez, Estrada, and Alvirez, 1973.) Many of
the studies that have been conducted on
fertility and immigration in the Mexican origin
population in the last two decades have
concentrated on either immigration (Cornelius,
1978; Portes, 1979) or fertility (Bean and
Bradshaw, 1977; Uhlenberg, 1973), without fully
examining the interrelationship of immigration
and fertility.

The literature on Mexican American
immigration has generally focused on the size of
the immigrant population or on its impact on
labor markets. The issue regarding the number
of immigrants has centered on the number of
illegals in the United States. Estimates of the
illegal population range from 12 million persons
(Chapman, 1976; Lesko Associates, 1975) to more
reliable estimates of 1.1 to 3.8 million (Bean,
King, and Passel, 1983; Warren and Passel,
1987). Labor market issues have focused on
whether illegal immigrants are taking jobs and
wages from U.S. Citizens (Borjas, 1982;
Grossman, 1982, 1984).

The fertility literature on the Mexican
American population has emphasized differential
fertility rates between Mexican Americans and
other groups. Bradshaw and Bean (1972) showed
that Mexican American fertility has exceeded
that of the Anglo population for at least 125
years. Their historical evidence indicates that

2

in 1850, Spanish-surname women in Bexar County, Texas had 32 percent more children under age five than did non-Spanish surname white women. From 1850 to 1950, Mexican Americans experienced a fertility decline parallel to that of the rest of the American population, but fertility levels remained much higher than those of other whites. Rindfuss and Sweet (1977) estimated that the total fertility rate (TFR) for Mexican Americans was 37 percent higher than the TFR for other whites in 1957-59, and 46 percent higher in 1967-69. Using data from the 1976 Survey of Income and Education, Bean, Swicegood, and Linsley (1981) found the mean number of children under age 15 to be 37 percent higher for Mexican American women aged 20-34 than for other whites. In 1980, the mean number of children ever born for Mexican origin women surpassed that of other white women by 44 percent (Bean, Stephen, and Opitz, 1985). A few demographic studies have examined other social factors leading to these group differences in fertility. Swicegood et al. (1988) determined that English proficiency and usage have a negative effect on cumulative fertility of Mexican American women, and that language factors interact with the level of female education in their effect on fertility. Fischer and Marcum (1984) found support for pronatalist subcultural norms, which resulted in higher Mexican American fertility.

While several studies have examined the connection between migration and fertility, most of the research has concentrated on movement from rural to urban areas within a country's boundaries. However, the present study examines data from both Mexico and the United States in order to investigate fertility behavior among Mexican immigrant women in the United States. The fertility levels of Mexican origin women according to their age and nativity status are examined in order to discern fertility patterns that are otherwise obscured when looking at the Mexican origin population as a whole.

3

THE JUNCTION OF IMMIGRATION AND FERTILITY

This research links two demographic processes in order to determine the short- and long-term effects of immigration on fertility in the Mexican origin population. The short- and long-term effects should be apparent, respectively, by examining current (children under age three) and cumulative (children ever born) fertility measures. The long-term effects would reflect changes in fertility behavior that continue throughout the childbearing years and would be expected to be seen in lower cumulative fertility, particularly for women nearing the end of their childbearing years. On the other hand, short-term effects are behavioral changes that occur only around the time of the actual immigration and are expected to be most evident in reduced current fertility, but not to be evident in specific age groups.

This research compares levels of current and cumulative fertility of Mexican immigrants with those of native-born Mexican origin women, and both immigrant and native-born Mexican origin women to non-Spanish origin white women. By further disaggregating the Mexican women by nativity, it is possible to discover the timing and changes in fertility of Mexican origin women as they are exposed to the fertility norms and values of the United States. Historically Mexico has maintained very high fertility rates; women immigrating to the United States are expected to have fertility norms and values reflecting the higher fertility of Mexico. As the immigrants attain socioeconomic positions in the United Sates similar to those of the native-born population, it is expected that they will acquire the norms and values of the host country.

This study seeks to determine what factors, such as age, immigrant status, and country of education, might have on the immigrant's acquisition of the U.S. fertility norms. There are several ways of dividing the Mexican origin

4

population in order to discern differences in fertility patterns. For instance, acculturation of norms and values is mediated in part by the age of the woman. Young immigrant women are expected to assimilate the new norms and values faster because the younger women have been in the childbearing years for a shorter period of time and have been exposed to the higher fertility norms of Mexico for less time. Therefore, current and cumulative fertility among the younger women should reflect the acceptance of the lower fertility norms.

Another factor that could influence the assimilation process is the status by which the immigrant entered the United States. It is likely that legal immigrants differ from illegals both in terms of socioeconomic status in Mexico, and the number and level of contacts made with the non-Hispanic population in the United States. Thus, by distinguishing in a very rough fashion among legal aliens, illegal aliens, and naturalized citizens, it is possible that different patterns of assimilation might be evident. Naturalized citizens are the most likely to have assimilated and would be expected to have the lowest current and cumulative fertility of these three groups as they have taken legal steps to be a part of the United States. The illegal aliens would be the least likely to have assimilated as their move may be seen as temporary and/or their contacts within the United Sates may be limited initially to interacting primarily with other Mexican origin persons (Jones, 1984). Illegals may be most affected by frequent and longer periods of spousal disruption (Browning and Cullen, 1983). Therefore, immigration would be likely to have short-term effects on the fertility of illegal immigrants and should be apparent in current fertility measures.

The assimilation of norms and values is also mediated in part by where the woman received her education. One of the primary sources of the transmission of norms and values

5

is education, and it is possible that women educated in Mexico have higher fertility norms than U.S.-educated women. This study examines the immigrant women by country of education to determine its effect on the assimilation of fertility norms.

This study also examines two aspects of the immigration process itself that may affect assimilation. The first issue is selectivity. If positive selectivity is present, women emigrating from Mexico may be non-representative and have fertility norms that are more similar to U.S. fertility norms. Selectivity is expected to have long-term effects because the characteristics associated with selectivity should remain in place over time. A second issue is disruption, which may occur in one or more forms. There may be long periods of spousal separation prior to or following the actual migration. Disruption is expected to have a short-term effect, evident around the time of the actual migration. Cumulative fertility may not reflect the disruption effect, if it is for a short period of time and/or the immigrant may actually make up for previously delayed childbearing.

This research, then, is concerned with whether assimilation explains fertility patterns of Mexican American women, given the confounding factors of immigrants status, country of education, selectivity, and disruption. Also the examination of two fertility measures makes it possible to distinguish the short-term from the long-term effects of immigration on fertility.

It is at the crossroads between Mexico and the United States where this research begins, just as immigrant women must choose crossroads on the journey and face the crossroads of culture as they adapt to life in the United States. The paths are varied and many, adding to the richness of this immigrant group.

CHAPTER 2

AN OVERVIEW OF THE MEXICAN ORIGIN
POPULATION IN THE UNITED STATES

It is important to examine the history of
Mexican immigration to the United States in
order to understand the socioeconomic position
of Mexicans relative to other immigrant and
native-born groups. This historical overview
also clarifies why the present-day Mexican
American population is heterogeneous in many
respects. The settlement of Mexican Americans
begins in the 1800s, when what is now primarily
the Southwestern United States passed into the
control of the United States by various means.[1]
Thus, the establishment of Mexican Americans has
been portrayed by some as a colonial system,
which differed from the voluntary European
immigration settlement pattern (Moore, 1970;
Murguia, 1975), while others have found evidence
that the long-term immigration of Mexican
Americans has not followed a pattern of
colonialism (McLemore and Romo, 1985).

The history of Mexican immigration to the
United States begins with the Spanish, whose
first settlement in the Southwest, the de Onate
Settlement, was established near Santa Fe in
1598. By 1630, the Spanish had established a
series of settlements and 25 missions
(McWilliams, 1968). All the original
settlements were destroyed in 1680 by Indian
attacks and, as a result, the Spaniards left New
Mexico. In 1692, Spanish explorer De Vargas
resettled the area and made peace with the
Indians. Spanish settlements spread to Arizona
in 1687 and, in 1775 and 1776, Juan Batista de
Anza led expeditions to California, where the
Spaniards eventually established 21 missions in
California, spread out from San Diego to San
Francisco.

As the Mexicans moved into the Spanish-held
Southwest, their settlement pattern resembled

7

the ribs of a fan (Moore, 1970), which spread
from California to Texas. Because the entire
region was sparsely occupied, the first settlers
formed small towns in strategic areas with
access to water and protection from Indian
attack. The estimated 120,000 Indians far
outnumbered the less than 75,000 early Mexican
settlers (McWilliams, 1968). The volume and
settlement pattern of the Mexicans varied by
state and by time of immigration.

TEXAS

The primary Spanish missions in Texas were
San Antonio, La Bahia, and Nacogdoches.
Although the Spanish spent three million pesos
between 1722 and 1744 in an effort to colonize
Texas, the population actually declined. A
peaceful transition from Spanish to Mexican rule
occurred throughout the Southwest following
Mexico's independence from Spain in the spring
of 1821. On July 19, 1821, a ceremony was held
in San Antonio to establish the villa's
allegiance to Mexico. As news of Mexico's
independence reached other cities, they joined
San Antonio in pledging their allegiance to
Mexico. Some Mexican officials were concerned
about the United States establishing settlements
in the Southwest, but others hoped that the
American settlers would encourage international
trade.
One of the Mexican government's first
actions regarding the Southwest was the passage
of the Imperial Colonization Law in 1823 that
allowed Americans who accepted the Roman
Catholic faith and become Mexican citizens to
settle in Texas. This law was annulled a year
later in favor of a second law that guaranteed
foreign settlers land, security, and exemption
from taxes for four years. These provisions
were particularly beneficial to Americans living
there, including the approximately 3,000
Americans living illegally in Texas at the time
(Weber, 1982). The law did not require

8

colonists to become Catholics or Mexican citizens, but gave land preference to Mexican citizens.

In 1821, Mexico granted land on the Brazos river to Moses Austin in exchange for bringing 300 Catholic families from Louisiana to settle in Texas. Following his death later in that same year his land title passed to his son, Stephen F. Austin, who by 1825 had brought 300 families into Texas, and eventually 900 families joined them under the terms of three additional contracts.

Two other successful colony leaders (empresarios) were Green de Witt and Martin de Leon who settled east and southeast of San Antonio. The "American Mexican" settlers were expected to ameliorate relations between Mexico and the United States but, in fact, they assimilated poorly and soon became the majority.[2] A Mexican law was passed April 6, 1830 that closed U.S. immigration to Texas, but encouraged immigration from Mexico and Europe. However, Mexican officials realized it was impossible to guard against illegal American immigrants and, in May 1834, Mexican President Antonio Lopez de Santa Anna rescinded the anti-immigration section of the law.

The shift from federalism to centralism in the Mexican government began in 1834 when President Santa Anna ousted his own liberal vice president, Valentia Gomez Farias, and dissolved Congress. This was met by rebellion throughout Mexico and its territories. On November 7, 1835 delegates from several Texas communities assembled at San Felipe de Austin and made a conditional declaration of independence. Texas' independence was complete after Santa Anna's forces were defeated in March 1836. Texas remained an independent country until March 1845 when it was annexed by the United States.

In 1848 Texas, New Mexico, Arizona, California, Utah, Nevada, and part of Colorado, became a part of the United States under the terms of the Treaty of Guadalupe Hidalgo.

9

Inhabitants of these areas automatically became U.S. citizens unless they returned to Mexico within a year. Only 1,500-2,000 Mexicans returned to Mexico under this provision leaving an estimated 5,000 Mexicans living in Texas at the time of the Treaty (McWilliams, 1968).[3]

After annexation, many of the approximately 30,000 Anglos living in Texas established large cattle ranches, which were based on ownership of livestock, rather than land ownership. The invention of barbed wire in 1875 allowed ranchers to enclose their lands for the first time and gave further rise to the distinction between Anglos with large cattle operations and other Anglos and Mexicans who had small or middle-sized herds, but no land. Anglos also developed cotton plantations in Texas throughout the late 1800s and recruited Mexicans as wage laborers and tenants. Several mercantile cities in the Rio Grande Valley flourished at this time, inhabited primarily by Mexicans. Although a Mexican middle class developed in the commerce-based cities, Anglo land ownership still dominated rural areas with Mexicans providing cheap labor. Thus, by 1900 land ownership and economic positions were fairly well set in Texas.

NEW MEXICO

The settlement pattern in New Mexico was quite different from Texas. The population of New Mexico at the time of the Treaty of Guadalupe Hidalgo was 60,000, almost all of whom were Mexicans. A census taken in 1840 counted only 23 Americans living in New Mexico, seven of whom had become Mexican citizens (Weber, 1982). The vast majority of the population lived near Santa Fe or at the headwaters of the Rio Grande and Pecos rivers, thus avoiding the border warfare that was characteristic of Texas settlements. Settlers in New Mexico were discouraged, however, by the Apache raids that occurred in the vast open areas of the state until 1881 when safer passage could be made by railroad. Owing to the Indian raids and difficulty in travel, villages and settlements in New Mexico were very isolated, which led to cohesive family and village units.

Another characteristic of the Mexican population in New Mexico was a well-established class structure that included an entrenched ruling class consisting primarily of Spanish origin persons (<u>Hispanos</u>). The division between the rich (<u>ricos</u>) and the poor (<u>pobres</u>) was caste-like in its character, as well as embodying the properties of differentiation. The <u>ricos</u> had lighter skin and were more "Spanish" in appearance than the <u>pobres</u>. Ethnic tolerance remained high in New Mexico for a long time, partially owing to the Mexican majority and Mexican acceptance of Anglos into commerce and their families. Intermarriage was common between Anglo men and Mexican women, even across social class lines (Gonzalez, 1967). However, ethnic tolerance began to decline about 1900 when Anglos began to dominate mining, ranching, and the transportation industries, and the concurrent relegation of Mexicans to less dominant positions.

Questions of land ownership arose when American land laws were enforced by the territorial government in New Mexico. The land grants were based on Spanish law of use and occupancy, rather that ownership. Villages often did not have land titles in their possession and lacked funds to hire lawyers. As a result, a Court of Private Land Claims was set up in 1891 by the territorial government to examine all of the land claims; the confusion over Spanish and American laws resulted in cases dragging on for years and most lands eventually being sold or released to Anglos or the National Forest Service.

ARIZONA

The settlement pattern in Arizona was different still. In the seventeenth century the Spanish established a series of missions along the San Miguel, Altar, Santa Cruz, and San Pedro rivers in what is now the southern part of Arizona. Few Mexicans resided outside the missions because there was no protection from Indian uprisings and raids. McWilliams (1968) estimated that only 1,000 Mexicans were living in Arizona in 1848, almost all living in either Tucson or Tubac, which was later abandoned after an Apache raid.

Arizona was a poor state in the mid-nineteenth century. There was no trade, as occurred in New Mexico along the Santa Fe Trail, nor were there ports as existed in California. In 1868 the estimated Mexican population was just 2,000 (McWilliams, 1968). However, the development of mining in the 1880s required a large supply of laborers, so Mexicans were recruited to work in the mines. Nearly all of the mining towns were isolated company towns, with Mexicans and Anglos segregated occupationally, residentially, and even by shopping hours in the company owned stores.

CALIFORNIA

California was an inherently rich territory with natural resources, a mild climate, and harbors. The Franciscan missions prospered and the value of their lands and holdings was estimated at $78 million in 1834 (McWilliams, 1968). A ruling-class elite (the gente de razon) boasted of being of pure Spanish blood and maintained palatial homes in the presidial towns of San Diego, Santa Barbara, Monterey, and San Francisco. However, the elites were outnumbered about ten to one by the cholos: Mexican soldiers, craftsmen, and colonists (McWilliams, 1968).

12

The most important social and economic transformation in California prior to the Gold Rush was secularization of the missions that began in 1832 and ended in 1845. Secularization was authorized by the Mexican Constitution of 1824, but was not fully instituted until 1836. Californians took over the provincial government in 1836 and under Alvardo's governorship (1836-1842) mission lands were sold or leased to private individuals. The land sales were undertaken to benefit three groups: the government in the form of land taxes, the Indians who could then obtain land, and the missionaries who were "guaranteed" a subsistence. The Spanish padres, who had controlled the land holdings, lost their authority as well as their land to the rancheros, some of whom controlled land holdings of 300,000 acres or more (Pitt, 1966). In 1843, Mexican Governor Michael Micheltorena called a moratorium on secularization, but his successor, Governor Pico liquidated the missions. The final sale of mission property was in May 1845 (Pitt, 1966).

The Mexican population in California (Californios) numbered only 7,500 at the time of the Treaty of Guadalupe Hidalgo (McWilliams, 1968). The Anglo population also was quite small, with 120 Americans in California in 1830. By 1840 that number had increased to 380 (Weber, 1982). Nearly all the Mexicans were males and, as in New Mexico, intermarriage of Mexican men and Anglo women was not uncommon. Political and economic connections with Mexico were weak and Mexico expressed little interest in major Mexican settlements in California before the Gold Rush.

The discovery of gold in 1848 brought 100,000 miners a year to the area. An estimated 13,000 Northern Mexicans (Sonorans) and Chileans joined the rush in 1849 (Moore, 1970). As a result, ethnic clashes were created and the Latin American immigrants faced the consequences of a lawless frontier and the miners'

13

xenophobia. Vigilantes drove away Chileans, Mexicans, and Peruvians from Sutter's Mill in 1849 and later a raid was held along the Sacramento River. Many of the Latin Americans fled to their homelands or San Francisco. The California State Assembly voted to ask the U.S. Congress to bar all foreign persons, even naturalized citizens, from the mines (Pitt, 1966). However, the crushing blow to the Latin Americans was the Foreign Miners' Tax Law of 1850, which was instituted by the state of California and required foreigners to buy monthly mining permits at a cost of $16. The foreigners left the mines, and the Anglos' profits dropped immediately. The tax was repealed in 1851 but, by that time, many of the Latin Americans had returned to their home countries and new immigration was very low.

As the profitability of the mines decreased, miners began squatting in large numbers on the Californios' ranches. By 1850 Californios comprised only 15 percent of the population, which resulted in loss of economic and political power (McLemore and Romo, 1985). Many of their land holdings established under Spanish rule were tenuous in the American legal system and many of the Californios lost most of their holdings through decree of the California Board of Land Commissioners.

Following the secularization of the missions in Southern California, land was owned by a few powerful Mexican rancheros with Indians providing labor. Based on state reports, Pitt (1966) found that 200 families owned 14 million acres of land ranging from 4,500 to 50,000 acres. Squatters did not bother Southern California ranches, as they disliked the climate, and the area remained without ethnic conflict until the late 1860s and early 1870s. Southern Californios suffered from a flood in 1862, followed by a two-year drought.

However, the primary force in the destruction of the area's equilibrium was the railroad, which reached San Francisco in 1869 and Los Angeles in 1877. The trains brought 120,000 Anglos to California in 1887, which can be contrasted to 12,000 Mexicans living in all of Southern California, and made local landowners the minority population almost overnight (Pitt, 1966). Land fights ensued and many of the ranches passed on to Anglos and Anglo business ventures.

Thus, at the turn of the twentieth century, the Mexican population in the Southwest had been inundated by Anglo settlers and had lost almost all of its political and economic power and land to the Anglos. By 1900, with the possible exception of New Mexico, Mexican Americans occupied a subordinate position in most of the Southwest (McLemore and Romo, 1985). Even at the turn of the century the number of Mexicans living in the Southwest was not large, making them a numerical minority as well as a discriminated-against minority.

1900-1929

A massive change occurred in the southwestern United States shortly after the turn of the century that had a profound effect on Mexican immigration. Large scale irrigated farming, which employed a large number of immigrants, began after a series of dams and reservoirs for the area were authorized in the Reclamation Act of 1902 (Moore, 1970). The Elephant Butte Dam alone brought 80,000 new acres into cultivation in the El Paso Valley; Mexican immigrants provided 90 percent of the labor that brought the land into cultivation (Reisler, 1976).

By 1929, the Southwest was responsible for 40 percent of the United States' total fruit and vegetable output (Reisler, 1976). The new crops such as melons, grapes, sugar beets, and lettuce were very labor intensive and the demand for cheap labor grew accordingly. Railroads linking the Southwest to the Midwest and the East assured farmers of markets, while canning and more advanced food preservation techniques assured higher quality products for the consumer. Cotton plantations that spread from Texas into New Mexico, Arizona, and the Imperial Valley in California also needed cheap labor.

Employment agencies operating primarily out of El Paso recruited up to 2,000 Mexicans per month for six-month work contracts (McWilliams, 1968). The Great Western Sugar Beet Company spent $360,000 recruiting Mexican laborers in 1920, and at least 30,000 Mexicans were brought to Colorado for weeding and harvesting sugar beets between 1910 and 1930 (McWilliams, 1968). Although the working conditions on many farms, railroads, and mines were often deplorable, wages ($1.00 to $1.50 per day) were up to five times higher than those offered in Mexico at that time (McLemore and Romo, 1985).

In 1900 the Mexican origin population in the Southwest consisted of 71,062 Mexicans in Texas, 14,172 in Arizona, 8,096 in California, and 6,649 in New Mexico (McWilliams, 1968). There were 31,118 official, or legal immigrants, from Mexico to the United States between 1900 and 1909 (U.S. Bureau of the Census, 1960), but Gomez-Quinones (1974) estimated that there may have been 50,000 unofficial immigrants arriving yearly, of whom 25 to 33 percent did not return to Mexico. Almost all of the immigrants settled in the Southwest and by 1930 the number of Mexican immigrants had risen to 114,173 in Arizona, 368,013 in California, 59,340 in New Mexico, and 683,681 in Texas (McWilliams, 1968).

The political situation in Mexico was unstable in the early 1900s; President Porfirio Diaz's land policy helped foreign investors and the Mexican elite to acquire lands that had been communally owned by peasant villages. Diaz's dictatorial regime ended in 1911 and was followed by full-scale revolutions for more than a decade in which more than a million people lost their lives (McLemore and Romo, 1985). Relations between Mexico and the United States worsened in the border towns because of raids into Mexico and the United States led by General John J. Pershing and General Pancho Villa respectively.

There was also a great deal of worker conflict in the United States in the 1910s. Strikes occurred in agricultural, mining, and railroad settings such as the 1915 miners' strike that included 5,000 Mexicans in three Arizona mines. Mexican workers of the Los Angeles urban railway struck in 1920. Agricultural strikes involving Mexican workers had begun in Ventura, California as early as 1903.

The outbreak of war in Europe interrupted the flow of European immigrant workers to the United States just as agricultural production was increasing in the Southwest. A new stream of Mexican immigrants met this demand for labor with over 63,000 legal Mexican migrants arriving in the United States between 1916 and 1920.[4] The peak annual number of Mexican immigrants during that era was 89,336 in 1924 (U.S. Bureau of the Census, 1960). Although U.S. immigration was altered greatly by the quotas prescribed in the 1924 Immigration Acts, Mexico was exempted from the quota system after effective lobbying from employers of Mexican laborers in the Southwest.[5] Almost immediately following the passage of the immigration quotas, organized labor leaders such as Samuel Gompers called for Mexicans to be added to the quotas list. The ensuing depression, however, automatically cut the demand for Mexican immigrants.

World War I and the depression of 1921-22 increased the rate of urbanization in the Mexican population in the U.S. By 1930, more than half of the Mexican origin population lived in urban areas including Midwestern industrial cities such as Gary, Detroit, and Chicago (McWilliams, 1968). This urbanization had positive and negative effects. For the first time, some Mexicans were able to learn skilled trades and escape the trap of being unskilled workers. However, the Mexicans generally still

17

occupied the lower rungs of the economic ladder; their housing and living conditions often reflected their status. The rapid urbanization in a few southwestern cities also created slum areas or <u>barrios</u> segregated from the Anglos.

1930-1964

The Great Depression hit the Mexican origin population hard, in both rural and urban areas. As the public welfare rolls swelled, public officials found it cheaper to send Mexicans back to Mexico than to keep them on welfare. Officials used both deportation and repatriation to return people to Mexico. Deportation required a legal hearing, while repatriation was "voluntary." Approximately 500,000 persons of Mexican origin returned to Mexico between 1929 and 1935 through deportation or repatriation (Hoffman, 1974). Raids held in major cities tended to be non-discriminatory as to citizenship status, and Mexican Americans were deported along with the Mexican nationals. The intimidation and fear of being deported kept many Mexican Americans from applying for public assistance to which they were entitled (McLemore and Romo, 1985).

The Mexican origin population also suffered in rural areas. When cotton in Texas became unprofitable, large numbers of cotton pickers were no longer needed; Anglos from the Dust Bowl states who migrated to California took away many of the unskilled agricultural labor jobs from the Mexican origin population. Also, wages dropped dramatically and small ranchers were unable to compete with larger, mechanized ranches. Other farmlands were taken out of production and no longer needed farm workers. As a result, many rural Mexican workers were forced to move to urban areas to find any kind of work and avoid starvation.

Following the Great Depression, the Mexican origin population was in a much better economic position, as some Mexican Americans broke out of

the previous system of unskilled farm and ranch
work. Their children could be educated in the
urban areas and the cities provided greater
opportunities for learning a skilled trade.
Also, some of the 300,000 to 500,000 Mexican
Americans who served in World War II learned
skilled crafts and trades in the service, and
increased opportunities in defense industries
existed for others at home (Moore, 1970).

The need for labor during World War II was
partially offset by large numbers of women who
joined the labor force, but not all positions
could be filled with domestic labor. The
employment situation was exacerbated by
improvements in the Mexican economy, creating
less of an economic push for Mexican nationals
to emigrate to the United States. As a result,
the U.S. and Mexican governments established a
program to bring Mexican national laborers to
work on the railroads and in agriculture.

Organized to follow specific guidelines
including safe working conditions, free
transportation, food for the laborers, and
guaranteed wages, the Bracero Program was set up
as a wartime program and was popular both with
Mexican laborers and American farmers. In its
first four years, over 167,000 workers came to
the United States (Barrera, 1979), and it was so
successful that it was continued until 1964. A
total of 4,914,156 Braceros came to the United
States during the program's 22-year existence
(Barrera, 1979). The program also benefitted
the Mexican government, which used the migration
as a safety valve for its development crises.

U.S. employers, particularly large growers
in California, were pleased with the program
because they received a steady labor supply and
government assistance in paying wages.[6] The
program was generally beneficial to the workers,
although there were certainly instances where
the terms of the contract were not upheld and,
by law, workers had to return to Mexico even if
they wished to remain in the United States.
Domestic workers did not benefit from the

program. Although employers were required to
hire domestic workers if they were available,
employers also sought to get around this and
hired cheaper laborers from Mexico. Also, farm
wages declined for all laborers in California,
primarily harming the native-born workers.

As a result of the economic recession
following the Korean War and increased numbers
of illegal immigrants coming to the United
States, the Immigration and Naturalization
Service instituted "Operation Wetback." From
1954-1959, 3.8 million illegal Mexican
immigrants were returned to Mexico (Murguia,
1975). As had occurred during the Great
Depression raids, anyone who even looked Mexican
was subject to harassment by U.S. Immigration
officials.

1965-1989

Mexican immigration over the last nearly
twenty-five years generally has continued
earlier patterns of immigration. The two
primary reasons for recent as well as past
immigration have been economic and family
reunification. In a sample of apprehended
undocumented Mexican aliens, North and Houstoun
(1976) found 75 percent had come to the United
States to seek work. Tienda (1981) and Portes
(1979) interviewed recent legal immigrants from
Mexico--many of whom had previously been illegal
aliens--half of whom came to the United States
seeking a job, and an additional 25 percent for
family reunification.

The number of legal and illegal Mexican
immigrants in the United States has been
discussed at length in both scholarly and
popular literature. The number of legal
immigrants is fairly well documented by the U.S.
Immigration and Naturalization Service. Between
1961 and 1970, 453,937 legal immigrants came to
the United States from Mexico and 492,046 came
between 1971 and 1980 (U.S. Department of
Justice, 1981). The number of illegal

immigrants appears to have increased throughout the 1970s, but estimates of the actual number of illegals have varied widely. Estimates as high as 8-12 million have been made by Lesko Associates (1975) and by Chapman (1976), but these estimates generally have been dismissed by those who have relied on empirical data. Siegel, Passel, and Robinson (1980) estimated that there were 3-6 million total illegals in the United States in 1980, of whom as many as 4 million might have been from Mexico. Bean, King, and Passel (1983) utilized Mexican and U.S. census data to analyze actual and hypothetical age/sex distributions of both countries and concluded that there were 1.5 to 3.8 million Mexican illegals in the United States in 1980. Bean and Tienda (1987) also estimated the number of undocumented Mexicans in the United States, using various undercount rates. In agreement with other estimates, they concluded that the maximum number of Mexican illegals in the United States in 1980 was 3.8 million, and it was likely much smaller than that.

Over the last twenty-five years, United States immigration policy has attempted to impose stricter control on immigration from Mexico. The 1965 Immigration and Naturalization Act moved away from the quota system based on national origins to a system limiting immigration to 120,000 persons from the Western Hemisphere. In 1976, the Immigration Act was amended to further limit immigrant visas to no more than 20,000 per country. The visas are issued under a preference system that emphasizes family reunification, and requires individual labor certification for all but a few categories of occupations.

The Immigration Reform and Control Act of 1986 (IRCA) was passed with the intent of reducing the number of illegal migrants, allow those who had been in the United States for five or more years the opportunity to become citizens, and to place responsibility on

21

employers to ascertain the legality of workers. This legislation was the product of four and a half years of debate in both the Senate and House of Representatives, and was patterned after legislation introduced in the 1980s by Sen. Alan Simpson (R-Wyo.) and Rep. Romano Mazzoli (D-Ky.). The Immigration Reform and Control Act of 1986 was signed into law by President Reagan on November 6, 1986.

One of the main features of the IRCA legislation was to provide amnesty through a legalization process for persons who met certain criteria. Persons would be allowed to adjust to permanent residence over a three-year period during FY89-91 if they lived in the United States continuously since January 1, 1982, filed for amnesty between May 5, 1987 and May 4, 1988, had no major infectious diseases, and could pay a filing fee of $185 per adult, $50 per child, or $420 for a family of 3 or more. After filing, persons are lawful temporary residents with work permits. If they continuously reside in the U.S. for the following 18 months and have no record of conviction for a felony or three or more misdemeanors, they may apply for permanent resident status after demonstrating ability in basic English and knowledge of the U.S. government.

In addition, persons who worked in perishable crops for at least 90 days during each of the years 1984-86 may adjust to permanent status after one year in a temporary status. Also, agricultural workers who worked for 90 days in the year prior to May 1, 1986 may also apply for temporary resident status, but must wait two years to apply for permanent residence (Montwieler, 1987). In addition, a replenishment program will be initiated in FY90 to bring in agricultural workers as needed to avert labor shortages. The determination of the need will be determined jointly by the Secretaries of labor and Agriculture.

Over 1.7 million persons applied for residency status through the pre-1982 provision

of the IRCA legislation, and an additional 1.3
million agricultural workers applied. Thus, all
told, the official number of immigrants admitted
to the U.S. will more than double from an
average of just over 600,000 persons per year to
approximately 1.6 million persons per year in
FY89-91 because of the adjustment of aliens
through the IRCA.

Preliminary analysis of the pre-1982
applicants indicates that 55 percent are male,
and 84 percent of the agricultural workers are
male (Singer, 1988). About 20 percent of the
pre-1982 applicants overstayed their non-
immigrant visas and approximately 80 percent
entered the U.S. illegally, that is without INS
inspection. Mexico is the primary country of
origin: 70 percent of the pre-1982 applicants
and 83 percent of the agricultural workers were
from Mexico. The second largest group (of the
pre-1982 applicants) were Salvadorans, followed
by citizens of Guatemala, Colombia, the
Philippines, Haiti, Nicaragua, Poland, the
Dominican Republic, and Iran. Applicants from
all other countries comprised 11 percent of the
pre-1982 applicants (Singer, 1988).

More than half (55 percent) of the pre-1982
applicants lived in California at the time of
their application, followed by 18 percent in
Texas, 7 percent in (each) New York and
Illinois, and 3 percent in Florida.

A PROFILE OF THE MEXICAN ORIGIN POPULATION: 1980

The Mexican origin population in the United
States increased from 4.5 million persons in
1970 to 8.7 million in 1980 (Bean, Stephen, and
Opitz, 1985). This near doubling of the
population was mainly a result of: 1) improved
coverage of the population in the 1980 Census;
2) increased immigration from Mexico; and 3)
high rates of natural increases.[7] Although the
vast majority (83 percent) of the Mexican origin
population lives in the Southwest (Arizona,
California, Colorado, New Mexico, and Texas),

the largest percentage increases in this
population generally were in states outside the
Southwest, excluding states with less than
50,000 Mexican origin persons. The five states
with the largest percentage gain were Florida
(280.0), Illinois (155.0), Washington (142.0),
Colorado (100.0), and Ohio (99.0) (Bean,
Stephen, and Opitz, 1985). Nonetheless, the
Mexican origin population as measured in
absolute numbers continued to be greatest in the
Southwest and Illinois, and continued to be
highly urbanized, with 87.6 percent living in
urban areas in 1980 (U.S. Bureau of the Census,
1983a).

Bean, Stephen, and Opitz (1985) have shown
that the sociodemographic characteristics of the
Mexican origin population imply a socioeconomic
position intermediate to that of blacks and non-
Hispanic whites. Their study found that labor
force participation is higher for Mexican origin
males (79.7 percent) than for either other white
(76.0) or black males (66.7). However,
unemployment is lowest for white males, with
Mexican origin males intermediate. The Mexican
origin population still shows signs of job
segregation with only 21.1 percent of Mexican
origin males in white collar jobs, compared to
45 percent of non-Hispanic white men. Studies
by Massey (1983), and Massey and Mullan (1984a)
have shown that blacks are more residentially
segregated from Anglos than are Hispanics.

SUMMARY

This brief historical overview of the
Mexican origin population in the United States
has focused on the timing and size of
immigration flows from Mexico, the settlement
patterns, the integration of the various
cultures, and U.S. immigration policies. Each
of these factors is relevant to considerations
about whether the Mexican origin population is a
conquered group, a group that is maintaining its
own heritage and culture while accepting parts

24

of American culture, or a group that is assimilating into the United States culture, or some combination of all of these. The following chapter further examines these kinds of issues in order to establish the context within which the hypotheses of this study will be developed.

CHAPTER 3

EVIDENCE FOR ASSIMILATION THEORY AND ITS APPLICATION TO FERTILITY RESEARCH

In choosing the most appropriate theoretical approach for a study such as this, it is critical to understand how a process such as immigration may affect historically diverse and socially or economically heterogeneous populations, such as the Mexican origin population.

Three frameworks that have been utilized in other studies of immigrant behavior are assimilation, colonialism, and cultural pluralism. The assimilation model is dynamic in its approach, allowing for systematic behavioral changes within an immigrant group. Colonialism and cultural pluralism models are both static in nature, but are opposites in terms of the relationship of the immigrant group to the majority. In the colonialism model, an immigrant group is seen as unequal to the majority group, unless there is a total revolt by the immigrants, in which case inequality still exists. Cultural pluralism, on the other hand, views immigrants as having equality with the majority and, therefore, there would be no need for immigrants to alter their behavior. The assimilation model is the only one of the three that allows for immigrant groups to alter their economic and political position through behavioral changes, and will be argued to be the most relevant framework to examine the factors affecting fertility change in the Mexican origin population in the United States.

COLONIALISM

Murguia (1975) has set forth 10 characteristics of the colonial model represented as an ideal type:

26

1) A militarily strong group conquers a
    people and takes over their territory.
    The conquered are of a different race, as
    well as different cultural and national
    backgrounds.
2) The conquerors are more technologically
    advanced.
3) The conquerors have economic and
    political control over the indigenous
    population.
4) The culture, heritage, language, and
    customs of the colonized people are
    labelled inferior.
5) A group of the colonized people are given
    some privileges in return for
    controlling their group.
6) The contacts of the colonizer and the
    colonized remain at a secondary level.
7) The colonized people eventually reject
    the colonizers, after having been
    rejected for structural assimilation.
8) There is a revival of their heritage,
    language, ethnic, and racial pride among
    the conquered group.
9) Warfare and harassment toward the
    dominant group is intensified.
10) The colonized people eventually take over
    their own lands and oust the colonizers.

In order to decide on the applicability of
the colonial model for this study of the effect
of immigration on fertility, it is useful to
first determine how closely the broad Mexican
American experience fits the ideal type. It is
evident from the historical events detailed in
the previous chapter that although the
settlement pattern of the Mexican population
varied from state to state, it was not one of
being conquered.
     The major battles in Texas were not caused
by a strong outside military group attempting to

27

conquer the area, but by the inhabitants seeking independence from Mexico. California was annexed on July 7, 1846 when men from three U.S. ships rowed across Monterey Bay and demanded the surrender of the capital of Alta California and the officials offered no resistance. In New Mexico, General Stephen W. Kearny led his exhausted troops into Santa Fe on August 18, 1846 and raised the U.S. flag over the Governor's Palace. New Mexican officials and citizens also offered no resistance. It is questionable that many in the Southwest felt much allegiance toward Mexico; there was little resistance toward annexation and little animosity or sense of being conquered.

Neither was there a definite or immediate shift in political power. In California and Texas, the shift was gradual and Mexicans retained power in certain areas, such as the Lower Rio Grande Valley in Texas. New Mexico has remained a political stronghold for Mexican Americans. Miguel Antonio Otero was the first Mexican American territorial governor of New Mexico (1897-1906). Statehood had been an issue in New Mexico for years and when a constitutional convention was finally held in 1910, 35 of the 100 delegates were Mexican American (Weber, 1973). New Mexico became a state in 1912 and the constitution declared that all the rights granted by the Treaty of Guadalupe Hidalgo would remain in effect. English and Spanish were equal languages for all state business, officially making New Mexico a bilingual state.

Murguia's definition of the ideal type of colonialism does not discuss the size and distribution of the conquered group; this would appear to be an important factor in assessing the relevance of colonialism. At the time of the Treaty of Guadalupe Hidalgo, the 250,000 American Indians living in the Southwest constituted the largest ethnic group in the area (McWilliams, 1968). There were relatively few Mexicans living in all of the Southwest (68,000) at that time and their settlements were scattered. The growth rate in the Southwest was quite high during the nineteenth century.[1] New Mexico's rate of natural increase (2.1 percent) was modest in comparison to Texas', but was nearly twice that of Mexico at the same time (Weber, 1982).

Growth was much more rapid in Texas prior to the Treaty, where it has been estimated that at least 1,000 Americans entered Texas per month in 1835 (Weber, 1982). Immigration resulted in an average annual rate of increase of 100 percent per year in Texas between 1821 and 1836. The border counties of Texas (Starr, Zapata, and Cameron) grew from 8,500 residents in 1850 to 50,000 in 1880 and then to 100,000 in 1910, with nearly all of the growth a result of continued immigration from Mexico (McWilliams, 1968). With the exception of Texas, where Mexicans were outnumbered by Anglos by about six to one in 1848 (McLemore and Romo, 1985), there were almost no Anglos in either New Mexico or California. No more than 150 Anglos entered New Mexico during the height of commerce on the Santa Fe Trail, and McWilliams (1968) noted that most of them left as soon as they sold their goods and wares. As a result, the inhabitants of these states were almost entirely of Mexican/Spanish origin as late as 1870.

Thus it is difficult to support the colonialization model in the Southwest when the population of the area was so small and consisted of relatively few Anglos prior to, or following the signing of the Treaty of Guadalupe Hidalgo. It was not until the twentieth century that large numbers of Mexican immigrants, who should be considered voluntary migrants, came to the United States. As recently as 1980, 26.0 percent of the Mexican origin population was born in Mexico (U.S. Bureau of the Census, 1983b). Overall, the colonial model may describe the Mexican population at the time of initial contact with the United States, but is not an accurate description of the Mexican

29

origin population's experience in the United
States since that time.

CULTURAL PLURALISM

Another perspective regarding the effect of
immigration is cultural pluralism, which was
fostered by Horace Kallen as a specific ideology
to preserve ethnic cultures, mother tongues, and
religions in order for groups to maintain some
of their distinctive cultural background. He
argued that every immigrant group was partially
assimilated in that they shared the English
language and had a common political system.
However, Kallen proposed a "federation of
national cultures" where language and political
structures would be common to all, but groups
should be able to maintain some of their unique
culture. Immigrant groups in the United States,
particularly non-English speaking groups,
settled in segregated neighborhoods in many of
the large industrial cities in the Northeast and
Midwest and created ethnic enclaves in these
cities.
Murguia (1975) has described cultural
pluralism as occupying a middle position on the
continuum between assimilation and colonization
and described its ideal type as:

1)   Two distinct ethnic or racial groups
     find themselves living side by side
     within a single political and economic
     unit (country).
2)   The groups keep most of their primary
     relations within their own group, but
     do participate in secondary relations
     with each other.
3)   Intermarriage is discouraged but not
     forbidden.
4)   Each group mutually respects each
     other's customs, culture and language.
5)   The groups are equal in political and
     economic power and influence.
     Equilibrium is maintained with neither

30

group gaining political or economic
advantage over the other.

The key to this model is that the groups have
equal political and economic power and that
there is little mixing of the two cultures.
    Based on Murguia's criteria for an ideal
type, cultural pluralism describes the Mexican
origin experience only moderately well. For
instance, there is little evidence that
intermarriage has been or continues to be
discouraged, particularly in certain localities.
Also, the Mexican origin population has not
reached economic/political equality with the
non-Hispanic population. Although the economic
position of Mexican Americans is continually
increasing, wages are still lower for Mexican
Americans than for non-Hispanic whites (Bean,
Stephen, and Opitz, 1985). Also, the small
number of Hispanic representatives in national
and state legislative bodies still does not
reflect the true number of Mexican Americans as
a percent of the total population (Welch and
Hibbing, 1984). Cultural pluralism may also be
rejected for this study because it is not clear
how to measure the "success" a group has in
reaching cultural pluralism. While cultural
pluralism may be a useful notion in terms of
describing an ideal, it has little power in
explaining how this ideal is reached by an
immigrant group.

ASSIMILATION THEORY

    The third perspective considered here is
assimilation. One of the earliest expressions
of assimilation theory was Park's sequential
theory of contact, competition, accommodation,
and eventual assimilation.[2] Groups come into
contact with one another through migration;
competition is created over natural resources,
goods, and services. Competition eventually
subsides as one of the groups establishes
dominance over the other and finally the groups

co-exist with a common culture. Park regarded
the cycle as progressive and irreversible,
"...diverse processes to be regarded as merely
the efforts of a new social and cultural
organism to achieve a new biotic and social
equilibrium (1950:104)." He also proposed that
while the tempo of the cycle may be slowed, it
is not possible to change or reverse its
direction.

Assimilation theory was further refined
when Gordon (1964) classified the roles that
race, religion, and national origin play in the
assimilation of groups. Gordon gave
assimilation theory a stronger base as a formal
theory of social change, distinguishing seven
variables or subprocesses in the assimilation of
immigrant groups:

1) Cultural assimilation or acculturation
2) Structural assimilation
3) Marital assimilation or amalgamation
4) Identificational assimilation
5) Attitude receptional assimilation
6) Behavior receptional assimilation
7) Civil assimilation

The first three elements of assimilation
are of critical importance and are central to
the remaining four elements. Gordon
hypothesized that all of the stages or
subprocesses take place in varying degrees and
at least some of the stages could occur out of
sequence. As Murguia (1975) noted, if
amalgamation or large-scale intermarriage has
occurred, then it can be assumed that at least
some identificational, attitude receptional,
behavior receptional, and civil assimilation
already has occurred.

Cultural assimilation or acculturation is
likely to be the first of the types of
assimilation to occur when an immigrant group
settles in the host country, and it is possible
for cultural assimilation to take place even
when none of the other types of assimilation

32

occurs. According to Gordon, this condition of
"acculturation only" could continue indefinitely
and has characterized non-Caucasians in America
(Murguia, 1975). Gordon hypothesized that
ethnic and racial groups generally undergo
fairly rapid cultural assimilation, which Warner
and Srole documented in their Yankee City series
(1945). Gordon also allowed that the
acculturation process may be slowed by some
intermediary factors such as: 1) spatial
isolation or segregation in rural areas, and 2)
pervasive discrimination, particularly if
institutions such as the educational system
participated in the discrimination.

Gordon concluded that the key to
assimilation and acculturation is structural
assimilation, because once it occurs all other
subprocesses eventually will follow. While
acculturation does not necessarily lead to
structural assimilation, acculturation is an
inevitable product of structural assimilation.
Gordon proposed that the process of structural
assimilation occurs for adults in primary
relationships or group settings such as clubs
and associations, but implied that work
associations are secondary relationships that
would not facilitate this process.

Murguia argued, however, that primary
relationships do exist within a workplace and
that the process of structural assimilation
could occur in such a setting. He further
stated that much of structural assimilation
occurs among adolescents and young adults rather
than within adult relationships. Primary
relationships are frequently formed at all
levels of schooling. School years are likely to
be the most formative ones for an individual,
and these primary relationships may be more
influential in the assimilation process than are
primary relationships formed later in adult
life. Education may bridge gaps in the
acculturation process, through desegregation of
schools, and the removal of at least some of the
spatial isolation in rural areas.

Inter-group marriage is another element of assimilation. When couples intermarry, cultural assimilation among children is almost automatic. Structural assimilation also will probably occur as primary relationships with relatives of the two ethnic groups will exist for the couple and their children. As discussed above, the other four processes of assimilation can be expected to have occurred prior to intermarriage or to follow shortly.

Although evidence indicates that certain ethnic groups such as Mexican Americans have not been successful in "translating their educational attainment into occupational prestige" even by the third generation (Neidert and Farley, 1985: 848-849), the assimilation model frequently has been conceptualized as a three-generation process (McLemore and Romo, 1985). In this conceptualization, the first-generation immigrants attempt acculturation, but nevertheless retain their ethnic identity. The second-generation--those born in the host country of immigrant parents--is more successful in the assimilation process. They learn the host culture's language, attend schools, and adopt the culture of the new country. Structural assimilation generally is completed in the second generation. In the third-generation--grandchildren of the immigrants--the assimilation process is virtually completed.

One might argue that it is difficult to utilize Gordon's framework because the assimilation process is difficult to quantify. However, four measures that have been used to approximate the degree of assimilation are language usage, intermarriage rates, occupational distribution, and educational attainment.

Ethnic groups in the United States have attempted to maintain their language, but among most European immigrant groups, English has become the primary language by the third-generation. Grebler, Moore, and Guzman (1970) found that a majority of a sample of Mexican

Americans living in Los Angeles and San Antonio
were bilingual. They also found that those with
higher incomes were more fluent in English than
lower-income persons, yet across income groups
many preferred to speak Spanish in the home.
There is some indication that the Mexican origin
population has retained Spanish longer than
would be expected in the assimilation process
(McLemore and Romo, 1985), owing in part to
contact with new Mexican immigrants and
bilingual education programs in the public
schools. Still, a recent study found that 50
percent of the Spanish mother tongue Hispanic
Americans use English as their primary language,
and more than 20 percent of the Hispanic
population reported in 1976 that English was
their mother tongue (Grenier, 1984).

Language may be used as an indicator of
human capital. That is, in the United States,
English proficiency may give access to job
opportunities that are available only to persons
who are fluent or at least bilingual. English
proficiency, as a proxy for opportunity costs,
would be expected to be negatively related to
fertility, particularly for Mexican origin women
in the labor force. Swicegood et al. (1988)
found that the effect of English proficiency on
current and cumulative fertility of Mexican
origin women was negative and increased with
rising education. The effects of English
proficiency tended to cumulate with age, and the
strength of the interaction between education
and English proficiency was greatest in the
youngest ages.

Another factor of assimilation is
intermarriage. The contemporary intermarriage
pattern of Mexican Americans reflects the
geographic patterns of the nineteenth century,
but the rate of exogamy has been increasing. In
Albuquerque, where intermarriage was fairly
common in the nineteenth century, the exogamous
marriage rate increased from 14 percent in 1915
to 39 percent in 1971 (Murguia and Frisbie,
1977). Similarly Grebler, Moore, and Guzman

35

(1970) found a 40 percent exogamy rate in Los
Angeles in 1963, compared to 17 percent between
1924 and 1933. In contrast, Alvirez and Bean
(1976) reported a rate of 9 percent in 1971 in
Edinburg, Texas. Grebler, Moore, and Guzman
(1970) did find that the third-generation
Mexican Americans are the most likely to marry-
out, supporting the three-generational
hypothesis.

Another aspect of assimilation, secondary
structural assimilation, can be measured by
examining the occupational distribution of the
Mexican origin population. From 1900 to 1930
Mexican Americans held jobs in agriculture,
mining, and railroads. Since that time Mexican
Americans have been successful in moving toward
the occupational distribution of all other
workers. The percent of Mexican Americans in
professional occupations rose from 2.1 in 1950
to 5.6 in 1978 (McLemore and Romo, 1985), and
farm labor declined from 23.4 to 6.4 in 1980
(Bean, Stephen, and Opitz, 1985; McLemore,
1983).

Educational attainment is another measure
of secondary structural assimilation. Education
is an important indicator of a group's
occupational distribution and its ability to
move out of low-skilled, low-paying jobs. The
median years of school completed for first-
generation Mexican Americans rose from 3.8 to
6.1 years between 1950 and 1970, and completed
education increased from 7.1 to 10.4 years for
the second- or higher-generation (McLemore,
1983). Thus, although the Mexican American
population's educational levels remain lower
than those of non-Hispanic whites, major
improvements have been made in the last 30 years
and can be expected to be reflected in the
group's occupational distribution in the future.

It appears from these examples that
assimilation theory is representative of the
Mexican origin's experience in the United
States. McLemore and Romo (1985) found some
support for the colonial model, yet they

36

concluded, "Taken altogether the information presented concerning language use, political success, occupational mobility and intermarriage may be interpreted as offering general support for the immigrant analogy." Mirowsky and Ross (1984:560) also found support for the assimilation theory:

> There is much evidence of assimilation among Mexican Americans; successive generations are better educated, more likely to be bilingual or speak only English, more likely to have half or most of their acquaintances non-Mexican, know more about Anglo culture and less about Mexican culture, and live more within the traditions, institutions and ways of Anglo culture than of Mexican culture.

SUMMARY

As applied to the Mexican origin population, none of the perspectives presented here--colonialism, cultural pluralism, or assimilation--perfectly matches its ideal type. This is to be expected of any ideal type, so the researcher must choose the most appropriate theory for the study.

The colonization model, however, seems less relevant to the concerns of this study because the Mexican origin population in the Southwest was small until the twentieth century, and it is not evident how colonialism has affected the Mexican origin population in the 1980s. The population of concern for this study is almost universally comprised of ancestors of, or persons who voluntarily immigrated to the United States. Also, there is scant evidence that the Mexicans in the Southwest were opposed to being annexed by the United States, and there was not a sense of colonization among the Mexicans at that time.

Cultural pluralism also is not particularly relevant to this study. Mexican Americans have retained certain aspects of their culture, but it is not evident they have attained economic and political power equal to that of the majority population. It is not clear how that equality is attained in the ideal, nor once equality is reached, how it is maintained over time. Cultural pluralism may be useful for descriptive purposes, but does not provide the forum to pose questions or reach conclusions sought in a study such as this.

In opposition to Murguia placing cultural pluralism in a central position on a continuum between the colonial and assimilation models, it can be argued that both colonialism and cultural pluralism contain aspects of assimilation. Therefore, assimilation occupies a central position on the continuum. It is evident that assimilation is basic to cultural pluralism, for if groups did not at least partially assimilate, this theory would have to be renamed cultural separatism. There are also aspects of assimilation in colonialism; although the assimilation may not be voluntary, the conquered group is expected to adopt the language and customs of the conquering group.

Both colonialism and cultural pluralism are theories that describe an ideal type, but fail to allow for changes undertaken by an immigrant group once in the country. On the other hand, assimilation theory is more dynamic and specifies changes that occur in a systematic fashion. The portions of colonialism and cultural pluralism that address change overlap with assimilation theory.

Another theory that has been utilized is ethnic resiliency, which has been defined by Portes and Bach (1985: 286) as:

> The higher the education, knowledge of English, and information about American society, the more critical are the attitudes toward it and the

38

more common the perceptions of
discrimination.

They review ethnic resiliency as an alternative
or contrary theory to assimilation, in that
assimilation theory predicts that these same
variables result in more favorable attitudes and
less perception of discrimination. According to
Portes and Bach, time is another element that
differentiates assimilation from ethnic
resiliency. They view assimilation as a slow,
linear process of adherence and acceptance,
whereas ethnic resiliency allows for immigrants
to establish relationships outside their own
group soon after their arrival in the host
country, while maintaining bonds of solidarity
within their ethnic community.
        However, it could be argued that ethnic
resiliency and assimilation are more similar
than Portes and Bach view them. Gordon (1964)
did not view assimilation as a linear process
and proposed that after structural assimilation
was complete, assimilation could proceed in any
number of ways. Furthermore, ethnic resiliency
may describe an early stage of assimilation
rather than a separate process. That is, the
establishment of relationships outside the
ethnic community are a first step in adaptation
to the outside or core group. But, these
relationships are not the endpoint of an
immigrant's adaptation, as would be suggested by
ethnic resiliency. In summary, ethnic
resiliency is a viable approach, but it is
considered here as an early process in the
assimilation framework.
        Thus, based on theoretical arguments and
historical evidence of the Mexican American
population, the assimilation model is the most
relevant theory for studying the effects of
immigration on fertility, and changes in
fertility behavior that may occur once the
immigrant is in the United States.

CHAPTER 4

HYPOTHESIZED EFFECTS OF IMMIGRATION ON MEXICAN AMERICAN FERTILITY

Assimilation as used in previous studies predicts that the longer the immigrant families are in the host country, the more likely they are to be integrated into its political and economic structures, and thus to adhere to its norms and values.

Applied to the fertility of immigrants, the assimilation perspective predicts that native-born Mexican American women will exhibit fertility levels intermediate to those of Anglo and foreign born Mexican origin women. When subjected to tests for a number of high fertility groups who have immigrated to the United States, the assimilation hypothesis has generally received support (Bean, Swicegood, and Linsley, 1981; Ford, 1982). Perhaps, in an effort to assimilate structurally, the second-generation women have been noted to show fertility levels even lower than those of native-born women of native parents (Engleman, 1938, 1951; Goldscheider, 1965, 1967; Rosenwaike, 1973).

However, support for the assimilation hypothesis in the case of the Mexican origin population has not been consistent. Using data from the 1960 U.S. Census, Uhlenberg (1973) discovered almost no reduction in completed family size among second- or third-generation Mexican American women. Jaffe, Cullen, and Boswell (1980) observed an overall decline in fertility among Mexican origin women between 1960 and 1970, but found only small declines in the number of children ever born in three generations of Mexican origin women after controlling for age, education, marital status, and employment. Rindfuss and Sweet (1977) also adjusted for several socioeconomic and demographic variables and found that in 1970 current fertility was higher for Spanish surname

40

women born outside the United States than for native-born women. Bean and Swicegood (1982) also examined current fertility and reported that first-generation Mexican American women had higher fertility than second- or higher-generation women, as measured by the number of own children under the age of three.

A number of reasons may account for the apparent discrepancies in the above studies. One is that cultural factors may maintain high levels of fertility within the Mexican origin population. Evidence as far back as 1850 indicates that Mexican American women at that time had about one-third more children than non-Hispanic white women (Bradshaw and Bean, 1972). Rindfuss and Sweet (1977) estimated 1969 total fertility rates (TFR) and found that Mexican origin fertility was about 30 percent higher than that for non-Hispanic white women. Ventura (1983) reported a 1980 TFR calculated from vital statistics data that Mexican origin women had fertility levels 70 percent higher than other white women.

A second reason for the opposing findings is that cumulative fertility, as used in the Uhlenberg study, has not shown a decline, but studies utilizing current fertility (Rindfuss and Sweet, 1977) have shown declines. The difference in findings may be a result of period, cohort, or age factors, or some combination of these (Bean et al., 1984). Period factors influence fertility levels by increasing or decreasing the timing of births.[1] Period-related factors could be expected to influence the fertility behavior of all ages uniformly, if they were the only determinants of fertility levels. Third-generation Mexican American women would be most influenced by period related factors as they would be the group most likely to assimilate structurally and, thus, would be most affected by changes in social and/or economic factors.

Cohort factors could affect both younger and higher generational status women,

41

particularly if the decline was a result of increases in female labor force participation and/or educational levels (Mare, 1981; Smith-Lovin and Tickamyer, 1978). Age factors also could account for fertility differences if subcultural forces exert their influence at certain ages. St. John and Grasmick (1985) have found evidence of subcultural forces among blacks during early stages of childbearing, resulting in age at first birth to be lower for blacks than whites. It is imperative, therefore, for fertility studies of immigrant groups to distinguish generational status, and examine age groups separately to determine the degree to which age, period, or cohort effects are operating within the population.[2]

AN ELABORATION OF ASSIMILATION THEORY

Another reason for the disparate findings may be that the assimilation model emphasizes the processes an immigrant encounters once in the host country, yet largely ignores the processes leading up to the immigration. This study will elaborate on assimilation theory by incorporating a focus on the process of migration itself and its effect on Mexican origin immigrants. Three perspectives will be used to explain the temporary and long-term effects of migration of fertility: 1) the selectivity model, which emphasizes that migration is selective of women predisposed toward low fertility; 2) the adaptation and socialization models, which conceptualize the immigrant as responding to the fertility norms of the host population; and 3) the disruption model, which argues that the migration process itself accounts for the fertility differentials.
Gorwaney et al. (1989) and Kahn (1988) have examined the effects of these processes on fertility for several immigrant groups in the U.S. and found strong support for the assimilation hypothesis and some support for the selectivity hypothesis. Because this study

42

focuses on one immigrant group over a ten-year period, it will be possible to sort out more of the effects of immigration on fertility.

It has been documented that migration is selective on variables such as age, education, occupational motivation, and marital status (Chiswick, 1979; Shaw, 1975; Shryock, 1964; Thomas, 1938). Owing to distances involved and cultural and economic barriers, it is probable that international migration is even more selective than is internal migration. The selectivity model further argues that even when background characteristics have been controlled, fertility will be lower among immigrants than non-migrants (Goldstein and Goldstein, 1983).

This perspective assumes that the fertility of immigrant women would be lower than that of other women in the sending country, even if they did not leave the sending country. It also implies that the low fertility of the immigrant may be affected by the same rational, decision-making behavior that guided and motivated the migrant to move (Goldstein, 1978). Selectivity has a larger effect when the fertility levels in the sending and receiving countries are particularly divergent. When the fertility levels of the two countries are similar, selectivity loses much of its effect because the immigrant's characteristics will be similar to those of the population in the receiving country, and also to those of the sending country (Goldstein and Goldstein, 1983). Evidence indicates that sending country fertility levels exert less influence on positively selected immigrants with respect to the host country, in part because they adapt more rapidly to the receiving country norms (Kahn, 1988). This might tend to amplify the effect of selectivity when fertility levels in the sending and receiving countries are greater.

The assimilation model assumes that immigrants have higher fertility than women in the host country, and that adoption of lower fertility norms will occur only over a long

43

period of time. It is only after three or more generations that one might expect to see the acceptance of lower fertility norms. This perspective predicts that the less fertility norms differ between sending and receiving countries, the sooner the migrant will adapt to the receiving country's fertility norms.

The disruption model assumes that migration itself is disruptive as a result of either spousal separation or through social or psychological disruption, which lowers fertility (Bean and Swicegood, 1982). Carlson (1985) has shown that the disruptive effects on migration and fertility are clearly visible, but are temporary and finite. Thus, if the disruptive effects are short lived, the pace of childbearing may actually increase after the disruptive effect has diminished. Cumulative fertility will be lowered the longer the disruptive effect exists, but may not be affected at all if the disruption is only for a short period of time.

EVIDENCE FROM PREVIOUS STUDIES

The disruption, selectivity, and assimilation models have been investigated in a study by Bean et al., (1984) who used data from the 1970 U.S. Census Public Use Sample (PUS) to investigate generational differences in current and cumulative fertility for three generations of ever-married Mexican American women ages 20 to 44. They found that fertility of Mexican Americans tends to approach that of other whites in the third- or higher-generation, without controlling for the influence of any other variables. This pattern was strongest for the current fertility measure (children under three), and was also evident for cumulative fertility (children ever born). They also found that among second-and third- or higher-generation women, fertility was higher than for other white women at all ages, as indicated by a higher number of children ever born as early as

44

the 20-24 age group. Once control variables were added into the model, different patterns emerged.[3] First-generation Mexican origin women had low cumulative fertility, particularly in the two-youngest age groups (20-24 and 25-29). These groups had more than one-third fewer children ever born than other women. With the exception of the 20-24 age group, levels of current fertility declined with rising generational status.

Three possible explanations were proposed for the low fertility of the young Mexican immigrants. First, Bean et al. (1984) concluded that selectivity was not operating as a factor because immigrant women at older ages had high levels of current fertility. Low fertility levels were observed only among young women, most likely those closest to the actual time of immigration. Second, the possibility that Mexican women leave some children behind in Mexico when they migrate to the United States was examined. However, this possibility was also dismissed since cumulative fertility, as measured by the number of own children under 15, was higher for Mexican immigrants than for other Mexican American women in the youngest age group. Furthermore, when ratios of own children to children ever born were computed, uniformly high ratios across generational groups were found that were as high as the ratios for other white women.

The disruption perspective was considered next and received the most support. Cumulative fertility was lower among immigrant women than among second- and third- or higher-generation women across all age groups, but current fertility was lower only in the youngest cohort of women. This could indicate that fertility is disrupted initially by the migration, and that immigrants then recoup postponed fertility. The disruptive effect is large enough to be reflected in the number of children ever born throughout the reproductive years.

The disruption effect among Mexican immigrants has been noted in other studies. Tienda (1980) found that over 45 percent of male Mexican immigrants in the United States were married, but came to the United States alone. Opitz and Frisbie (1985) reported that 17.2 percent of recent male Mexican immigrants (arrived in the United States between 1975 and 1980) 25 to 34 years of age in 1980 were married with spouse absent, but did not report being separated. This figure jumps to 32.3 percent for the 35-44 year old recent male Mexican immigrants. The corresponding figures for females are not nearly as high (5.4 for 25-34 year olds and 5.7 for 35-44 year olds), but they are nearly three times as high as the next highest group. These two studies give support to the physical disruption hypothesis, whose effect on fertility may be exaggerated even more by emotional or mental disruptive effects.

The following section presents the study hypotheses integrating a number of issues that have not been resolved in previous studies. The assimilation model provides the basic framework for the hypotheses, but this research will elaborate on assimilation theory by focusing on the specific effects of selectivity, disruption, and adaptation on fertility of the Mexican origin population.

AN ELABORATION

Based on the theoretical considerations and empirical findings of previous studies, the following six tasks will be undertaken in the present research: 1) an examination of fertility levels within Mexico during the 1970s; 2) an analysis of first-generation women by year of immigration to the United States; 3) an application of the life cycle approach using age cohorts; 4) a comparison of fertility patterns of the first-generation women as categorized by probable immigrant status; and 5) an investigation of the effect of educational status on fertility by place of education.

Fertility trends in Mexico will be examined first in order to understand better the normative context from which the immigrant comes, and also to attempt to determine if the Mexican immigrants are a select population. As Rindfuss (1976) stated, the effect of migration on fertility is of most interest when the fertility norms and behavior differ between the place of origin and the place of destination.

As noted earlier, selectivity and assimilation operate as factors only when the fertility norms of the two countries are different. Furthermore, an examination of fertility levels is particularly important when fertility has declined recently in the sending country. Fertility declines across age groups in the first generation may reflect fertility declines in the sending country, rather than adaptation to the fertility norms of the receiving country. Mexican fertility trends will be examined to determine if selectivity of immigrants is occurring and if the fertility declines in Mexico during the late 1970s (Westinghouse Health Systems, 1978) have dampened fertility within the first generation residing in the United States.

The United States analysis will commence with an initial examination of the effects of selectivity, adaptation, socialization, and disruption on the fertility levels of foreign-born and native-born Mexican origin women. Utilizing data from the 1980 U.S. Census, current and cumulative fertility measures will be presented for the two generational groups and by five-year age groups. This allows for the determination of generational and/or age differences that may be obscured when merely standardizing or controlling for age differences or if generational status is not taken into account.

47

An examination of age cohorts from 1970 and 1980 by time of entry into the United States will be presented next. This is a critical analysis as Ford (forthcoming) has shown that analyses of immigrant fertility that do not consider duration of residence in the host country may be misleading. Current fertility in particular tends to be depressed around the time of the move, which is compensated for approximately 5-10 years later.

The timing of immigration in combination with a woman's age at time of entry is important because if a woman came to the U.S. in her late teens or early twenties, then fertility reductions would be expected to be concentrated in those ages. However, if a woman immigrates as a child or in her later reproductive years, the disruptive effect on current fertility would not occur. In order to address these life-course processes, it would be necessary to have complete fertility and migration histories. Unfortunately, that type of detailed information is not available anywhere for the Mexican origin population; however, time of immigration within five-year time spans is available from U.S. census data.

Year of immigration data allow for the separation of first-generation women into those who immigrated between 1975 and 1980 (recent immigrants) versus all other first generation women (earlier immigrants). Current and cumulative fertility then can be examined to detect the effects of selectivity, disruption, socialization, and/or adaptation for the most recent and earlier immigrants by age groups.

As seen in Figure 1, if disruption is operating as a factor it should be most evident for the recent immigrants by lowering current fertility. The number of children ever born (Figure 2) should be higher for earlier immigrants than that of other whites, as well as higher than that of recent immigrants, if immigrants later make-up for fertility postponed during the migration. Support for the

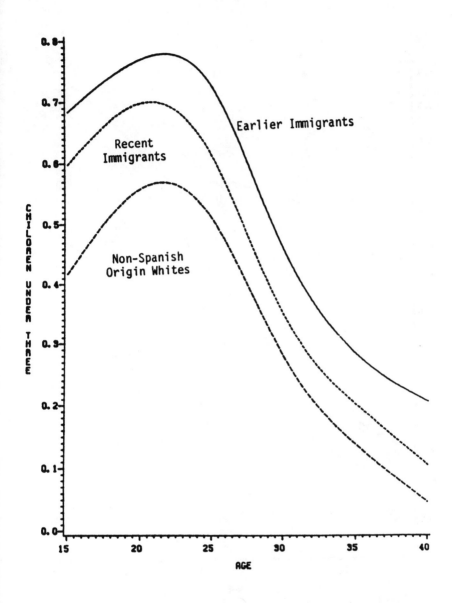

Figure 1.   Hypothesized Effects of Disruption on Children Under Three for Immigrant Women

49

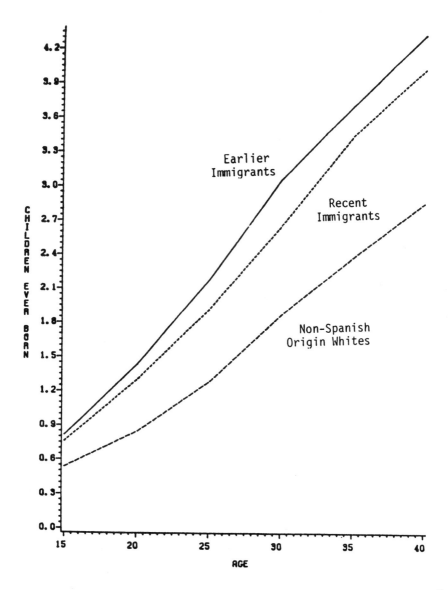

Figure 2. Hypothesized Effects of Disruption on Children Ever Born for Immigrant Women

50

assimilation hypothesis (Figures 3 and 4) would be found if fertility decreases from recent immigrants to earlier immigrants and may be most evident in the young ages where it is more likely that women in the first-generation would quickly accept the fertility norms of the United States.

Depictions of the selectivity hypothesis are shown in Figures 5 and 6, but utilize a different reference group than in the other sets of figures. In a comparison to other women at the place of origin, the selectivity hypothesis would be supported if both current and cumulative fertility were lower across all age groups for all immigrants than for non-immigrants. If selectivity were operating as a factor, fertility levels should be diminished at all ages and the characteristics associated with selectivity should remain in place over time, resulting in lower cumulative fertility even in the older age groups of the earlier immigrants. Since fertility levels remain so much higher in Mexico than in the United States, selectivity may not be apparent in a comparison of immigrants to other white women, even if the immigrants are a select group. Therefore, this study will examine the selectivity hypothesis both in terms of fertility levels at the place of origin and place of destination.

A related issue is the comparison of age cohorts from 1970 to 1980 to distinguish life cycle processes from other factors--such as selectivity and disruption--that may affect fertility. If there are particular cohorts that are predisposed toward lower fertility, then their fertility should remain depressed throughout their reproductive life cycle. Although it would be preferable to have observations at several points of time, data ten years apart should make it possible to determine cohort differentials that can be distinguished from other factors such as selectivity. A cohort effect would be present only in certain age cohorts, whereas fertility depressions

51

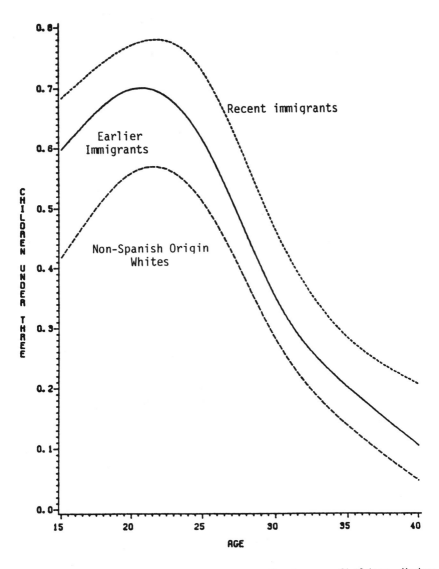

Figure 3. Hypothesized Effects of Assimilation on Children Under
Three for Immigrant Women

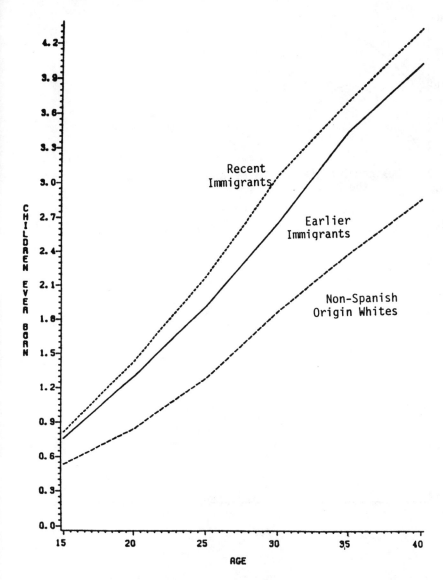

Figure 4. Hypothesized Effects of Assimilation on Children Ever Born for Immigrant Women

53

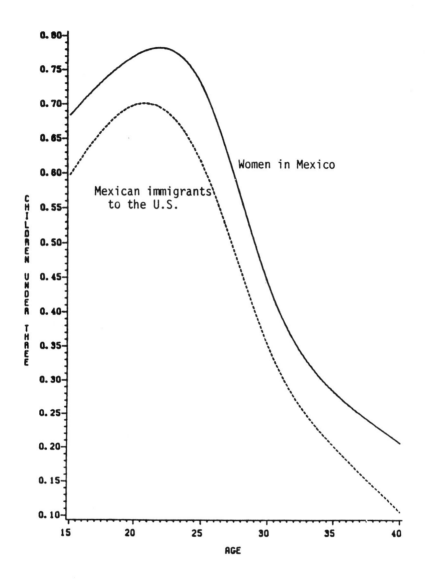

Figure 5. Hypothesized Effects of Selectivity on Children Under
Three for Immigrant Women

54

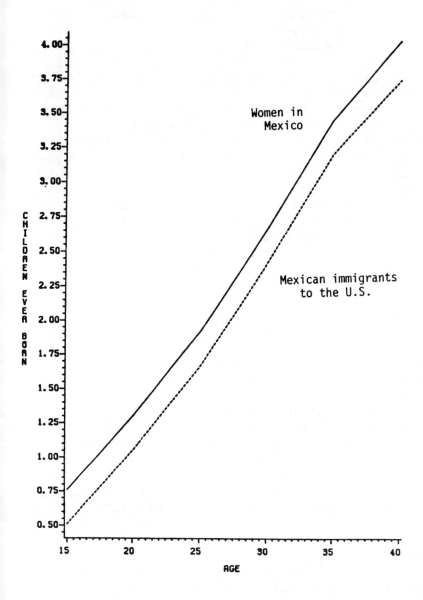

Figure 6. Hypothesized Effects of Selectivity on Children Ever Born for Immigrant Women

55

should be present uniformly across all age groups of the foreign-born women if selectivity is operating as a factor.

Another issue the present study addresses concerns the assumption of the homogeneity of the first-generation. This actually is a larger problem with the 1980 data than it was in previous years. The Mexican origin population in the United States increased from 4.5 to 8.7 million persons between 1970 and 1980 (Bean, Browning, and Frisbie, 1984). However, a major factor in this increase in 1980 was the inclusion of more than 1.1 million illegal immigrants from Mexico who were not included in the 1970 Census (Warren and Passel, 1987). Thus, it is important to distinguish among legal migrants, illegal migrants, and self-reported naturalized citizens in the first-generation.

Heterogeneity can only be partially addressed directly with census data, with some additional inference required. Bean, Browning, and Frisbie (1984) have examined the 1980 Public Use Microfile Sample and categorized the first-generation into three groups. Category I contains post-1975 immigrants who are Mexican born and not citizens of the United States. They estimate that this group is made-up of at least two-thirds undocumented immigrants. Category II is composed of pre-1975 immigrants who are Mexican born and not citizens of the United States. Based on an analysis by Warren and Passel (1987), Category II was estimated to contain over one-third undocumented migrants and nearly two-thirds legal aliens. The third group, Category III, consists of Mexican born persons who self-reported that they were U.S. naturalized citizens. Bean, Browning, and Frisbie (1984) estimate that approximately 35 percent of this group actually has achieved citizenship, while the remaining 65 percent are, in fact, not naturalized citizens. They may misreport themselves as citizens while they are in the process of achieving citizenship in the case of legal aliens, or because it is deemed to

56

be a safer response to a government document in the case of illegal aliens.

It is evident that this categorization does not provide a perfect distinction among undocumenteds, legal aliens, and naturalized citizens, but it is a means to examine the heterogeneity of the first-generation, and to determine what factors are operating to lower the fertility levels of the different immigrant groups.

The hypothesized effects of disruption, selectivity, and assimilation may be reexamined using this three-way categorization. Disruption is proposed to be the predominant factor in lowering fertility for the undocumenteds because it is more likely that these persons experience more frequent and longer periods of separation of spouses, in addition to the actual disruption of the move. Again, this pattern should be evident by lowering current fertility.

Cumulative fertility should reflect high levels of fertility already obtained in Mexico or fertility being made-up after the initial disruption. Selectivity is expected to be the predominant factor in lower fertility for legal aliens and an important factor for naturalized citizens based on Bean et al.'s (1984) findings of higher educational attainment, English proficiency, occupational distribution, and income for these three groups. It is expected that assimilation will also characterize the naturalized citizens, as they have already taken legal steps to become citizens. This factor may be partially muted because only 35 percent of the persons in this category are true naturalized citizens. If assimilation is operating as a factor, current fertility should be low. Cumulative fertility levels would be expected to be high to moderate, particularly in the older ages, reflecting initially higher fertility norms that are adjusted downward after residing in the United States.

Another important issue to be examined in this study is education. In previous studies, education has been found to be a primary control factor. Depending on when a woman immigrated, she may have been educated in Mexico where mean levels of education historically have been, and continue to be, much lower than in the United States, (Grebler, 1967; Mexico Instituto Nacional de Estadistica Geografia e Informatica, 1983). This study will attempt to determine where first-generation women received their education based on their age and year of immigration, and examine the differences in current and cumulative fertility levels by country of probable education for the first-generation women.

A final issue which deserves to be addressed here, but will not be discussed at length in this study, is a lack of information in the U.S. census data about the origin of the immigrant within Mexico. There is a large divergence between urban and rural fertility within Mexico (Browning and Feindt, 1969); it is evident that an immigrant from an urban area in Mexico will come to the United States with lower fertility norms than immigrants from rural areas. This is further complicated if the migration occurs in stages, that is, if a migrant moves from a rural area to an urban area within Mexico, and then immigrates to the United States. Unfortunately, the censuses do not contain background data on area of residence in Mexico, nor information on number of moves. This last issue is a critical one and, although left unresolved in this study, it is hoped it will be pursued in future studies.

RESEARCH HYPOTHESES

This research is primarily concerned with how the processes of selectivity, disruption, and assimilation influence the fertility behavior of Mexican immigrants in the United States. These processes are examined singularly, but are considered to be complementary rather than competing processes.

The research hypotheses are summarized in Table 1. This table shows three specific hypotheses that will be examined in connection with each process and indicates the mechanism through which it is expected that the fertility behavior of the Mexican origin women is affected.

Selectivity will be examined first because it must temporally precede both disruption and assimilation. Selectivity is assumed to exist prior to immigration and its effects are thought to remain in place following the move. Thus, a selectivity effect on fertility should be long term and would lower both current and cumulative fertility. Such an effect, however, may be confounded by changes in fertility norms and behavior occurring in Mexico during the late 1970s. That is, fertility may be lower for women who immigrated between 1975 and 1980 than for other first-generation women, but this may be caused by lower fertility norms of these recent immigrants, rather than selectivity.

Disruption is the next process to be examined as it occurs temporally prior to the assimilation process. Disruption is difficult to measure because we do not know the length of any physical separation of the spouses preceding or following the immigration, nor do we have available measures of the psychological strain that may be associated with immigration and that have consequences for fertility behavior. However, it is hypothesized that the disruptive effects of immigration will be short term, primarily evident in their impact on current fertility. Disruption may also lower cumulative fertility if Mexican origin women do not later make up for delayed childbearing.

The third process is assimilation, which is hypothesized to lower fertility among native-born Mexican Americans. The Mexican origin population is disaggregated in a number of ways to ascertain the mechanisms by which assimilation lowers fertility. One division entails a rough categorization of the Mexican origin population by immigration status. The

59

TABLE 1. Summary of Research Hypotheses

Selectivity

1. Immigration is selective of Mexicans who have higher socioeconomic
    status and education levels.

2. Mexican immigrant women will have fertility levels lower than
    those of women remaining in Mexico.

3. In addition to selectivity, fertility levels of women migrating to
    the United States between 1975 and 1980 should further reflect the
    lower fertility norms of Mexico, and have lower fertility than
    other Mexican immigrants who arrived prior to 1975.

Disruption

4. Owing to the physical and/or social disruption of the move,
    disruption will have the effect of lowering fertility around
    the time of the immigration.

5. The longer the disruption, the lower the fertility of the
    immigrants.

6. Mexican origin women partially make-up for their postponed or
    delayed fertility owing to the short-term effects of the
    disruption, but their cumulative fertility levels will continue
    to reflect the disruptive effect to some degree.

Assimilation

7. Fertility is lower with increasing time in the host country.
    Thus, native-born Mexican origin women are expected to have
    lower fertility than first-generation Mexican women.

8. Assimilation is expected to be a major factor in lowering
    fertility among legal immigrants and naturalized citizens, but
    disruption is expected to have a larger effect among illegal
    migrants.

9. Assimilation is expected to be most effective in lowering
    fertility among Mexican origin women who are educated in the
    United States.

60

Mexican origin population in 1980 is quite
different from that of 1970, so the effects of
assimilation and disruption are examined by
distinguishing among the three categories of
immigrant status to determine if assimilation is
more apparent among the predominantly legal
aliens and self-reported naturalized citizens.
Another analysis of the effect of assimilation
on fertility explores where the woman received
her education. Because school is an effective
means of instilling norms, it is hypothesized
that immigrant women educated in the United
States will have lower fertility than women
educated in Mexico, and women who received a
portion of their education in each country will
have fertility levels intermediate to the
Mexican-educated and U.S.-educated women.

In order to evaluate these various
hypotheses regarding immigration and its complex
role on altering fertility norms and behavior of
Mexican origin women in the United States, the
next chapter discusses the data sets used in
this analysis, and operational definitions are
presented.

CHAPTER 5

DATA AND METHODS

Three data sets are used in this study to investigate the hypothesized effects of immigration on fertility as presented in Chapter 4. This analysis utilizes information from the 1970 U.S. Census data, the 1980 U.S. Census data, and the 1976-77 Mexican World Fertility Survey (EMF). The following sections detail the study samples, definitions of variables, and methodological limitations of each data set. This is done first for the two U.S. censuses, then for the Mexican World Fertility Survey.

UNITED STATES SAMPLE

The basic data for this study are from the 1970 United States Census 1-in-100 Public Use Sample (PUS) state file (15 percent questionnaire) and the 1980 United States Census five percent Public Use Microdata Sample (PUMS-A). In 1970, only the 15 percent questionnaire contained the questions on nativity of parents and only the state file delineated the five southwestern states in which the Spanish surname identifier was used.

Ethnicity is defined in this study in terms of the woman's characteristics. In 1970, Mexican Americans were delineated in either of two ways. (See Hernandez, Estrada, and Alvirez, 1973, for a full description of the methods for defining the Mexican American population). Persons who designated themselves as "Spanish American" were included, except for Spanish Americans residing in New York, New Jersey, and Pennsylvania, as the Census Bureau considered Spanish Americans living in those three states to be Puerto Ricans. Spanish Americans living in Florida were classified as Cubans. The Census Bureau considered persons living in the five southwestern states--Arizona, California,

Colorado, New Mexico, and Texas—to be Spanish
American if Spanish was their mother tongue or
if they had Spanish surnames. In all other
states, persons were designated as Spanish
Americans if they were persons of Spanish
language. The second criterion was nationality;
if a person reported that they or one of their
parents had been born in Mexico they were also
considered to be Mexican American.

The Spanish origin question was asked of a
five percent sample of the population in 1970,
but for the first time was asked of everyone in
the 1980 Census. The question asked respondents
to self-identify whether they were of Spanish
origin or descent.[1] The origin of the
respondent's mother was used if the person
reported a multiple origin. Mexican Americans
were defined as "Mexican," "Mexican American,"
"Chicano," or those persons who wrote in an
entry such as "La Raza."

Non-Hispanic whites are defined in this
study as all other whites not of Spanish origin.
Various samples of the subpopulations of
interest are used in this study in order to have
a large enough sample for between and within
group comparisons. A 1-in-2,000 sample of non-
Hispanic households is utilized for both 1970
and 1980. While a 1-in-100 sample of the
Mexican American population is used for the 1970
data, two samples are utilized for 1980: a 1-
in-20 sample of possible illegals (persons born
in Mexico who were not U.S. citizens and arrived
in the U.S. between 1975 and 1980), and a 1-in-
80 sample of the remaining Mexican origin
population. (See Appendix A for a full
description of the sample.) Thus, the sample
sizes presented here do not reflect the
relationship in size between the Mexican origin
population and other whites, but the two
generations of Mexican Americans are in
proportion to one another.

The sample is limited in this study to
ever-married women aged 15 to 44 who are of
Anglo or Mexican descent.[2] In this study there

63

are two basic analyses using the U.S. Census
data: 1) comparisons of Mexican origin women to
other white women, and 2) comparisons of
immigrant Mexican women to native-born Mexican
origin women. In the exploration of
assimilation, the Mexican origin women are
compared to the other white women, while the
within the Mexican origin population group
comparisons are useful in determining what
factors alter fertility behavior as generational
status increases. Never-married women were
excluded because their fertility would be
expected to deviate from that of ever-married
women. Marital status is controlled in the
analysis to provide a large and representative
sample, while allowing for the effect of marital
disruption on fertility.

OWN CHILDREN MEASURES

The dependent variables for the majority of
this analysis are: children ever born
(cumulative fertility) and number of children
under age three (current fertility). The
distinction between cumulative and current
fertility is important and analogous to the
distinction between cohort and period fertility.
Cohort fertility is measured by the number of
children ever born to a group of women born or
married during a specific period of time.
Period fertility represents the number of
children born to all women during a given time
period such as one year. Thus, the two measures
of fertility may be affected by different
factors. For instance, period fertility may be
low in a given year owing to changes in the
aggregate timing of births, which eventually may
be made up and would not be reflected in the
overall cumulative fertility of a cohort (Bean
and Swicegood, 1985).
For this study, the number of children ever
born variable is taken directly from the two
censuses and period fertility is approximated
using own children measures, such as the number

64

of children under the age of three. For the own
children allocation, family relationships were
examined to match children to their mothers.
This allocation was undertaken by the Computer
Services Section of the Population Research
Center at the University of Texas under a
related research project, and has been detailed
in Bean, Swicegood, and Linsley (1981). This
procedure is designed to allocate children to
their social rather than biological mothers,
particularly for subfamilies within a household.
Children are allocated to women if two criteria
are met: 1) if the child and the woman have the
same family identification number, and 2) if the
detailed relationship recode of the child
corresponds to that of the woman. Therefore, a
child would be allocated to a woman if the child
was coded as the child of the family or
subfamily head and had the same family
identification as the mother.

A number of assumptions must be made when
using the own children data. Rindfuss and Sweet
(1977:11) have listed four of these assumptions
as: "1) that ages of children and women are
correctly reported, 2) that all children reside
with their mothers, 3) that mortality is
negligible for women and children, and 4) that
all women and children are covered by the
census." These criteria are important to the
current study since it is possible that there is
variation in their applicability among the
generational groups and the Anglos.

In order to evaluate the own children data,
a comparison was made of the own children under
age one to vital statistics data for the Mexican
origin and other white population as shown in
Table 2. It appears that the own children
method is quite accurate after age 19. The low
ratio for the 15-19 age group is probably a
result of children being put up for adoption,
whereas the high ratio in the 40-44 age group
may be caused by the presence of adopted
children and/or grandchildren being miscoded as
own children.[3]

TABLE 2. Census Estimated Fertility Rates and Recorded Vital
Statistics Rates for the Mexican Origin and Other White
Populations: 1980

	Mexican Origin			Other Whites		
	PUMS (1)	Vital Statistics (2)	Ratio of PUMS to VS (1)/(2)=(3)	PUMS (4)	Vital Statistics (5)	Ratio of PUMS to VS (4)/(5)=(6)
15-19	60.8	95.6	.636	24.6	41.2	.597
20-24	153.2	176.8	.867	106.7	105.5	1.011
25-29	151.7	147.1	1.031	117.2	110.6	1.060
30-34	96.6	95.2	1.015	76.1	59.9	1.270
35-39	56.3	48.4	1.163	18.8	17.7	1.062
40-44	18.4	14.2	1.296	5.6	3.0	1.867
TFR	2685.0	2815.5	.954	1745.0	1689.5	1.033

SOURCES: 1980 United States Census of Population and Housing, PUMS-A
file; and Ventura (1983:5).

The 1970 Census data did not designate subfamilies within a household, so a small number of women in the 1970 PUS may have been coded as childless, when, in fact, they may have had children living with them in that household. This downward bias is expected to be quite small as the Census Bureau stopped using the subfamily or secondary family designation because the number of such families was so small. Bean, Swicegood, and Linsley (1981) were able to allocate 98.8 percent of the eligible children with their mothers for the 1970 Census. Bean and Swicegood (1985) estimated that 99.3 percent were allocated using the 1980 data.

ANALYTICAL MODELS

In 1970, generational groups could be delineated on the basis of questions on the nativity of respondents and their parents. Nativity information available from the 15 percent questionnaire enables a three-generational classification. Women could be distinguished according to whether they were born in the Mexico (first-generation), whether they were born in the United States, but one or both of their parents were born in Mexico (second-generation), or whether they and their parents were born in the United States (third- or higher-generation). However, the 1980 Census did not ask birthplace of parents and in order to provide comparable results for 1970 and 1980, information will be presented only for the first-generation and second- or higher-generation.

Because generational status is a categorical variable, dummy variable regression models are used (Miller and Erickson, 1981). Generation is coded as a series of two dichotomous dummy variables: first-generation and second- or higher-generation. The Mexican origin women are given a score of 1 if they fall within a given generational group; the other white women are the reference group and are

67

given a score of 0 for each of the generation dummy variables. When scored in this manner, the estimates of the regression coefficients may be interpreted as the average deviation in fertility of that generational group from the mean fertility of other whites. When other variables are included in the model, the deviations may be interpreted as reflecting average differences, after adjusting for differences in other variables.

Multiple regression analysis is used to test the research hypotheses. This analysis requires that a number of socioeconomic and demographic characteristics are held constant in order to compare either the Mexican origin women to other white women or within the generational comparison of Mexican origin women since these groups may occupy very different socioeconomic positions and/or have different demographic characteristics. Multivariate statistical techniques allow for the possible confounding influence of such factors to be eliminated from the study of fertility differentials. The basic linear regression model utilized is:

$$F_i = a_0 + b_1 G_1 + b_2 G_2 + \Sigma C_j X_{ij} + e_i$$

Where F_i is the fertility of woman i, a_0 is the regression intercept, G_1 and G_2 are the generational status dummy variables, C_j is the regression slope for the jth control variable, X_{ij} is the score of woman i on control variable j, and e_i is the error term. The intercept represents the mean fertility of other whites, as they are the omitted or reference group for the two generation dummy variables. The Mexican origin women were coded 1 for the generational group in which they fell; the other white women were coded 0 for each of the two generation dummy variables. This model was estimated separately for each age group. Generational status was included first, then education, then the remainder of the independent variables were added.

68

MEXICO FERTILITY SURVEY

The Mexican data are from the 1976-77 World Fertility Survey (WFS), which was conducted by the Direccion General de Estadistica with the collaboration of the Institute of Social Research, Universidad Autonoma de Mexico, The Colegio de Mexico, the National Population Council and the Information System for Economic and Social Programming. Fieldwork was conducted between July 1976 and March 1977. Information was collected at three levels: 1) the community, 2) the household, and 3) the individual. The first questionnaire was asked of local officials and contained items such as number of inhabitants, government services, and types of economic activity. The other two interview schedules were completed with the sample households. The main purpose of the Household Schedule was to identify women eligible for the interview who were aged 20-49, or 15-19 years old if they had been married or had at least one live birth (World Fertility Survey, 1980).[4] Other questions on the Household Schedule included relationship to household head, place of birth, age, sex, and occupation for all household members. Information on fertility and mortality in the household in the last 12 months was also included to evaluate the vital registration system. The individual questionnaire utilized the WFS core questionnaire and family planning module, including a complete pregnancy history.

The sample for the Mexico Fertility Survey (EMF) was a subsample of the National Household Survey and was a nationally representative, multi-stage, stratified, clustered area sample, with a self-weighted design. The household sample was selected using two area stages for Mexico City, Guadalajara, and Monterrey and the other self-representing areas, with the first true sampling being at the block level (World Fertility Survey, 1981). Three area stages were

69

used to select the sample in the non-self-representing areas, including 39 primary sampling units (municipios). The sample contained 13,739 households of which 13,080 were successfully interviewed (95.2 percent). Approximately a one-in-two sample of women was taken within households, resulting in 7,672 selected women. The completion rate was very high (95.3 percent), and the main reason for non-interviews was absence of the respondent. The refusal rate was quite low at 0.5 percent. The final sample consisted of 7,310 women (World Fertility Survey, 1980).

A evaluation of the Mexico Fertility Survey was prepared by Manuel Ordorica and Joseph Potter (1981). They examined the internal consistency of the data collected and compared the results of the survey to independent sources of information. Age heaping was found around ages ending in zero and five, although the Myers' Index was only three-quarters as large as that of the 1970 Mexican Census. The EMF individual survey included a question on date of birth, which produced much less heaping than the question on age at last birthday. They concluded (1981:10) that "...age is relatively well reported in the individual survey." A number of checks were done on the nuptiality data including a comparison of the individual and household data, and fitting the three-parameter Coale marriage curve to the single-year data. They found a 97.9 percent match on nuptiality between the individual and household survey and, in addition, did not detect any bias in the selection of women for the sample based on marital status. In a comparison of other surveys to the EMF, Ordorica and Potter fit the Coale marriage curve to the EMF data and concluded that the data on nuptiality were quite believable and of good quality.

Another way of checking the nuptiality data was to compare the mean age at marriage with the mean age at first birth, resulting in average differences of about 15 months. The only cohort

that had a questionable figure was the 20-24
year old cohort with an average duration of 12
months. Ordorica and Potter analyzed the
fertility data primarily to determine the
accuracy of the pregnancy histories, but these
results are not of central concern to the
present study. Age-specific fertility rates
were calculated from the EMF maternity histories
and compared to birth registrations. Vital
registration is considered to be fairly complete
in Mexico, but a delay in reporting a birth is
not uncommon. In Ordorica and Potter's
comparison of EMF and vital registration, there
was a consistent pattern over time with larger
survey fertility rates than those observed in
the vital statistics in ages 15-19, small
positive differences from ages 20-29, high
positive differences from 30-34, then small
negative differences through age 45.

SUMMARY

        Three data sets will be used to explore the
hypothesized effects of selectivity,
assimilation, disruption, and other factors on
fertility. The empirical portion of this
analysis begins with an examination of
selectivity in Chapter 6. Using data from the
1980 U.S. Census and 1976-77 Mexican World
Fertility Survey, female Mexican immigrants to
the U.S. are compared to women remaining in
Mexico. In Chapter 7, data are utilized from
the 1970 and 1980 U.S. Censuses to examine
disruption and assimilation using generational
and cohort comparisons. The 1980 data are
utilized in the final empirical chapter (Chapter
8) to examine the effects of place of schooling
and immigration status on immigrant fertility.
It is evident that the diverse hypotheses of
this study can be examined in depth by utilizing
data sets for the two countries, and over a ten-
year time period for the United States.

71

CHAPTER 6

THE FERTILITY REVOLUTION IN MEXICO AND THE SELECTIVITY HYPOTHESIS

This chapter examines whether immigration is selective of women predisposed toward lower fertility. The logic of linking selectivity with lower fertility is based on:
1) immigration is costly and immigrants need financial resources to immigrate; 2) immigration is positively selective of persons, as measured by socioeconomic variables; and 3) women with higher socioeconomic status have fewer children (Bagozzi and van Loo, 1980; Janis and Mann, 1977; Schedlin and Hollerbach, 1981; Van Arsodol, Sabagh, and Butler, 1968). Therefore, based on the above assumptions, it is hypothesized that Mexican immigrant women in the United States will be positively selected on a number of socioeconomic variables as compared to women remaining in Mexico, and will have lower fertility than non-immigrant Mexican women.

In order to provide a socioeconomic and historical framework for the selectivity hypothesis, this chapter will highlight fertility trends in Mexico during the twentieth century, emphasizing the fertility decline recorded during the 1970s. This overview is important to understand the fertility context from which a Mexican immigrant comes and is of particular interest when fertility is declining rapidly in the sending country. The fertility declines that were experienced in Mexico during the 1970s would be expected to result in lower fertility of recent immigrant women in comparison to women who immigrated prior to the fertility transition in Mexico. Thus, selectivity may be confounded by the recent changes in fertility trends throughout Mexico, and this needs to be taken into account in this analysis.

Descriptive statistics of fertility trends in Mexico will be presented first to provide the

72

context for comparing Mexican and Mexican-American women. The population policies of Mexico will be considered next as they are integral factors in the fertility decline. Then, a sample of Mexican women will be compared to female Mexican immigrants in the United States to determine if immigration is selective of women with lower fertility norms at the country of origin.

RECENT TRENDS IN MEXICAN FERTILITY LEVELS

Mexico's population grew slowly from 1900-1940, as shown in Table 3. A negative growth rate recorded for 1910-1921 reflects the social and economic upheaval associated with the 1910 Revolution (Alba, 1982). Population growth accelerated beginning in the 1940s and peaked at 3.43 percent in the 1960s, a result of a rapid drop in mortality and stable fertility rates. From 1940 to 1970, the crude death rate dropped from 23.4 to 10.1 per thousand persons, and the crude birth rate declined from 44.6 to 44.2 (Alarcon, 1982). By 1980 the crude death rate was 6.3 and the crude birth rate was 36.3 (United Nations, 1986).[1]

Since the 1940s, Mexico has become increasingly industrialized with the Gross National Product averaging a steady growth rate of 6.5 percent per year (Alba, 1978). The industrial sector has grown, largely owing to manufacturing activity. In real terms, per capita income tripled between 1940 and 1980 (Pullum, Casterline, and Juarez, 1985).

In addition to industrial development, the demographic context needed to precipitate a fertility decline was in place by 1970. For instance, infant mortality dropped from 110.7 in 1944-46 to 68.5 in 1970 (Alba, 1982; Unites Nations, 1975). However, Mexican fertility levels did not decline as would have been expected by the demographic transition (Coale, 1978). Seiver (1975) found that, as of 1970, the crude birth rate was not masking age- or

Table 3. Average Annual Growth Rate, Mexico: 1900-1980

Years	Population	Average Annual Growth Rate (%)
1900	13,607,259	
1910	15,160,369	1.09
1921*	14,334,780	-0.51
1930	16,552,722	1.10
1940	19,653,552	1.72
1950	25,791,017	2.72
1960	34,923,129	3.13
1970	48,225,238	3.43
1980	67,382,581	3.33

SOURCE: Alba, 1982: 18.

*-The Mexican Census was taken in 1921 not 1920.

TABLE 4. Total Fertility Rates, Mexico: 1971-1979

Year	Total Fertility Rate	Yearly Decline (percent)	Decline from 1971 (percent)
1971	6.72	--	--
1972	6.67	.74	.74
1973	6.40	4.05	4.76
1974	6.13	4.22	8.78
1975	5.94	3.10	11.61
1976	5.42	8.75	19.35
1977	5.37	.92	20.09
1978	4.82	10.24	28.27
1979	4.68	2.90	30.36

SOURCE: Alarcon, 1982: 27.

*-For women age 15-49.

region-specific declines in fertility. He concluded that the demographic transition had not begun in Mexico, nor was it about to begin, because the crude birth rate even in the most developed state (Mexico D.F.) was 33 per thousand.

As shown in Table 4, Mexico experienced a dramatic and sustained decline in fertility during the 1970s. Fertility declined 30 percent over the decade, with the largest one-year decline (10.24 percent) recorded in 1978.

Fertility declines were not concentrated in certain age groups or certain localities. As seen in Table 5, fertility declines occurred in all age groups between 1971 and 1979. The age-specific fertility rates shown in Table 5 indicate substantial decreases in all ages. The primary reproductive age groups (20-34) showed the largest actual changes, and the oldest reproductive age groups (40-44 and 45-49) had the largest percentage declines (41.38 and 60.00 percent respectively).

Fertility declines were noted in rural, urban, and metropolitan areas during the 1970s, as seen in Table 6. Decreases in the Total Fertility Rate were consistent in each of the three areas. Rural fertility remained higher than urban and metropolitan fertility in 1979, but the rural fertility levels dropped substantially during the decade.

The crude birth rates for each Mexican state from 1940 to 1977 are shown in Table 7. It is evident that although fertility levels vary considerably among states, fertility declined in all states except Veracruz between 1970 and 1977. Thus, it is evident that fertility remained consistently high and stable in Mexico until the 1970s and then began to decline.

FACTORS IN MEXICO'S FERTILITY DECLINE

Classic demographic transition theory proposes that fertility will decline following

75

TABLE 5. Age-Specific Fertility Rates, Mexico: 1971 and 1979

Age Groups	Fertility Rates		Percent Change
	1971	1979	
15-19	.131	.103	21.37
20-24	.316	.220	30.38
25-29	.319	.225	29.47
30-34	.275	.186	32.36
35-39	.195	.142	27.18
40-44	.087	.051	41.38
45-59	.020	.008	60.00
Total	6.715	4.675	30.38

SOURCE: Alarcon, 1982: 28.

TABLE 6. Fertility Rates for Rural, Urban, and Metropolitan Areas, Mexico: 1971-1979

Years	Rural*	Urban	Metropolitan
1971-1973	7.60	5.42	5.26
1974-1976	6.86	4.67	4.36
1977-1979	6.00	3.79	3.53

SOURCE: Alarcon, 1982: 27.

* Rural areas include persons living in places of less than 2500 inhabitants;
Urban areas include persons living in places of between 2500 and 500,000 persons;
Metropolitan areas include inhabitants of Mexico City, Guadalajara, Monterrey and Puebla.

TABLE 7. Crude Birth Rates for Mexican States, by Broad Levels
of Fertility: 1940-1977

	1940	1950	1960	1970	1977
GROUP 1					
Distrito Federal	33.52	39.78	44.00	42.58	34.46
Mexico	49.39	48.52	49.05	36.46	29.44
GROUP 2					
B.C. Norte	40.83	44.30	46.02	41.78	31.87
Chihuahua	43.92	41.04	43.30	40.13	34.08
Nuevo Leon	44.48	42.39	45.55	42.40	34.36
Tamaulipas	37.86	44.16	43.88	39.58	34.05
GROUP 3					
B.C. Sur	39.45	40.51	40.41	43.53	36.41
Campeche	45.98	45.87	47.62	44.49	41.02
Coahuila	55.47	48.09	47.47	50.49	38.34
Colima	42.06	46.73	47.42	44.14	37.69
Chiapas	36.97	39.29	32.30	38.63	37.73
Jalisco	44.29	45.65	44.09	44.25	40.30
Morelos	44.96	44.14	46.96	41.87	38.82
Quintana Roo	31.82	40.28	32.16	53.27	37.48
Sonora	46.83	46.08	48.04	44.22	35.35
Veracruz	34.62	40.00	38.38	36.77	37.48
Yucatan	43.85	43.69	43.70	43.26	40.51
GROUP 4					
Aguascalientes	45.29	48.83	49.86	48.09	40.74
Durango	49.64	45.49	46.32	45.90	43.57
Guanajuato	55.56	48.49	46.13	43.91	38.30
Guerrero	41.48	44.74	47.64	46.57	43.60
Hidalgo	37.48	42.51	44.92	44.97	42.54
Michoacan	44.25	46.24	47.22	46.31	41.26
Nayarit	41.88	46.40	48.74	44.28	37.94
Oaxaca	41.19	40.93	42.49	43.60	42.05
Puebla	42.48	41.59	44.10	46.42	45.43
Queretaro	46.05	46.34	49.27	49.64	40.92
San Luis Potosi	50.55	46.61	49.15	46.69	40.75
Sinaloa	37.88	42.17	45.88	47.94	41.72
Tabasco	37.87	43.26	46.76	44.33	41.36
Tlaxcala	50.57	48.59	50.01	51.44	49.61
Zacatecas	52.97	53.04	50.93	47.91	40.19

SOURCE: Ordorica, 1984:94.

reductions in mortality and increases in industrial development. However, the declines in mortality and increases in development preceded the fertility decline in Mexico by a number of years. Although there is no question that decreases in mortality and increased development were factors in the fertility decline, there are additional reasons for the decline in the 1970s. One primary factor was the population policy changes throughout the decade (Garrison, 1984). Another major reason for the fertility decline was concomitant changes in the intermediate variables (Pullum, Casterline, and Juarez).[2]

Hernandez, Porras, and Zuniga (1982) examined a number of the intermediate variables that might have had an impact on the decline such as the percent of women marrying and using contraceptives. They found virtually no change in the proportion of women married between 1970 and 1980 and that the proportion remained high; differences in the proportion marrying therefore, were not a factor in the decline. In their analysis of marital fertility rates, Hernandez, Porras, and Zuniga (1982) concluded that the variations observed in the total fertility rate between 1970 and 1979 were due to declines in the marital-specific fertility rates in women 15 to 44 years of age. Therefore, declines were a result of women altering their fertility behavior within their marriages and not a result of a decrease in the proportion of women marrying.

Contraception is one of the primary ways for a woman to alter her fertility behavior. In 1982 contraceptive usage was reported by 4.5 million women in 1982, 25 percent of all Mexican women of childbearing age (Covarrubia and Gonzalez, 1982). Hernandez, Porras, and Zuniga (1982) found that women who had never used contraceptive methods had nearly 1.5 more children than women who had used contraceptive methods at some time. As seen in Figure 7, contraceptive usage began to have an effect on

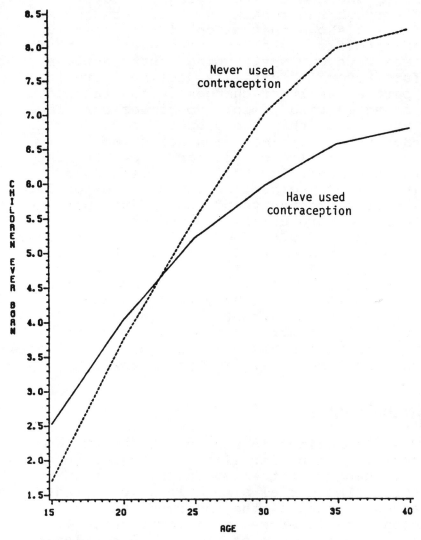

SOURCE: Hernandez et al., 1982: 254.

Figure 7. Children Ever Born by Contraceptive Status, Mexican
Women: 1979

79

the number of children ever born in the 25-29 age group, and had an increasingly greater effect through the remaining childbearing years.

Table 8 shows that except for ages 15-19, marital-specific fertility rates were lowest for women who were currently using contraceptives.[3] Therefore, overall fertility declines were in large part a result of changes in contraceptive usage among married women. Rodriguez-Barocio et al. (1980) found that the proportion of legally or consensually married women using family planning methods increased from 42 percent in 1976 to 56 percent in 1978. They also found that in 1976, 48 percent of the women exposed to the risk of a pregnancy and who did not want any more children were using a method of contraception in 1976, and within two years that proportion increased to 62 percent. Pullum, Casterline, and Juarez (1985) found that the fertility declines of almost five percent per year between 1977 and 1982 were due almost entirely to increased contraception. The availability of contraceptives was no doubt important in this behavioral change, and will be discussed in more detail in the following section.

POPULATION POLICY

The alterations in the social normative structure regarding fertility were met with parallel changes in the governmental normative structure. The social alterations were created by changes in some of the intermediate variables; the governmental alterations, however, were a result of changes in population policy. The reasons for the reversal in national policy never have been discussed publicly, but it is generally agreed that it was a result of concern about the consequences of rapid population growth in the wake of high inflation and economic crises (Warwick, 1982). The governmental policy changes were an abrupt reversal of the previous pronatalist policies

80

TABLE 8. Marital-Specific Fertility Rates, Mexico: 1979

Age Groups	Contraceptive Status		
	Current Users	Former Users	Never Used
15-19	.574	.358	.342
20-24	.334	.235	.411
25-29	.232	.244	.346
30-34	.134	.200	.304
35-39	.097	.196	.194
40-44	.038	.065	.057

SOURCE: Hernandez, Porras, and Zuniga, 1982: Table 4.

and required altering local environments by convincing individuals that low fertility was in the best interest of the entire country, as well as their own, and by making contraceptives available (Potter, 1983).

The Mexican legislature approved several changes to Mexico's population policy in 1973. The prohibition on advertising and selling contraceptives was lifted in the New Health Regulations Code passed February 26, 1973. The legislature also passed the General Population Law on December 11, 1973, which proposed: 1) reductions in mortality; 2) integrating women and marginal groups into national and economic development; and 3) implementing family planning programs. An important provision of the General Population Law established the National Population Council (CONAPO), an interministerial coordinating body that began operating in 1974. Article Four of the Political Constitution of the United Mexican States was published in the Official Gazette on December 31, 1973 and provided both a legal basis for family planning organizations, and the right for individuals to decide on the number and spacing of children. As reported in Alba (1982:104) this legislation states in part that:

> Men and women are equal before the law. This will protect the organization and development of the family. All people have the right to decide in a free, responsible and informed manner on the number of children they will have and at what intervals.

From 1974 to 1976 CONAPO coordinated and set up family planning programs that offered clinical services under the rubric of maternal and child health care. By 1976 about one million women actively participated in government programs, with another 100,000 women participating in private programs (Alba, 1982).

The next major family planning legislation
was passed on November 17, 1976. The broad
provisions of this law included family planning
in the context of social welfare policies, and
in health, education, and training. In October
1977, President Portillo approved the National
Plan for Family Planning. This plan established
short-, medium-, and long-term demographic goals
of 2.5 percent population growth by 1982, 1.9
percent by 1988 and 1.0 percent by the year
2000. The Office of Coordination for the
national Family Planning Program (CPF)--a new
agency established by this legislation--was
directed to implement the new policies.
Although family planning had been included in
the 1973 legislation, setting growth goals was a
major step in Mexico, particularly because the
President also directed the Secretariat of
Programming and Budget to incorporate the Plan
into the Overall Development Plan (Alarcon,
1982). Five general objectives of the National
Plan for Family Planning were:

1.   Promote and provide family planning
       services to encourage the improvement
       of the population's health conditions,
       to reduce mother-child morbidity and
       mortality, to promote the regulation
       of fertility and thereby reduce the
       birth rate throughout the country.

2.   Reduce the incidence of abortion by
       increasing family planning practices.

3.   Develop educational family planning
       programs for the health sector, in
       addition to formal guidance and
       information programs that will reach
       the entire population.

4.   Establish an infrastructure for
       administration and services that will
       allow for continuity and expansion in

family planning programs throughout the nation.

5.   Organize implementation services to adapt information, supervision, and assessment systems to the state and national level.

One chapter of the 1980-82 Overall Development Plan addressed demographic change within the broader topic of social change (Plan Global de Desarrollo, 1980):

The general objective of the demographic policy to establish guidelines for reproduction and migration that are more compatible with the new development model is only meaningful in terms of its relation to the overall development process, that is, the demographic growth goals are incorporated into the context of programming for health, education, housing, employment, human settlements and sectoral production.

Alarcon (1982:37) summarized the changes in Mexico's population policy as:

Mexico now has a clear and precise population policy with a solid legal basis in the Mexican Constitution itself and a National Plan for Family Planning based on the Constitution with demographic goals established up to the year 2000 and a related action program that is becoming increasingly institutionalized and integrated into the context of the nation's public health and general development.

It appears that the National Family Planning Plan has been successful to date. The short-term goal of 2.5 percent annual population growth was reached in 1981, ahead of the targeted date of 1982 (Covarrubia and Gonzalez,

84

1982). A number of unanswered questions remain regarding the timing of the fertility decline and what caused it. For instance, why didn't the decline start in the 1960s when the levels of development in Mexico had set the stage for fertility to drop? Also, was the implementation of family planning programs the major factor in the eventual fertility declines? If so, what accounts for the drop in fertility from 1970-1976? These questions remain unanswered at this time, but it is evident that women in all age groups and geographic areas of Mexico were affected by the fertility decline of the 1970s. We now turn to a discussion of selectivity of the Mexican immigrant population and how that might have been affected by the fertility transition of the 1970s.

THEORETICAL CONSIDERATIONS RELEVANT TO SELECTIVITY

Selectivity assumes that migrants are positively selected at the place of origin based on characteristics such as higher education, occupation, and mobility aspirations (Goldstein and Goldstein, 1983). As applied to fertility, the selectivity model states that even when all other relevant characteristics are controlled, migrants continue to have lower fertility than that of nonmigrants. This further implies that even if migrants did not move, their fertility would be lower than that of the remainder of the population.

Selectivity theory has emphasized push and pull factors at the place of origin and destination, respectively. Thomas (1941) established relationships between the economic cycles of Sweden and the United States with emigration from Sweden, by emphasizing the push factor originating in the Swedish economy. Others, however, have emphasized the pull factors of the country of destination (Easterlin, 1955; Jerome, 1926).

The migration stream from Mexico to the United States has been described as consisting of persons moving primarily for labor-related reasons (Alba, 1978; Portes, 1983). A labor-migration stream could be described as reacting to pull factors at the destination, push factors at the origin, or some combination of the two. Frisbie (1975) found in a longitudinal analysis that push factors had more importance than pull factors, particularly for illegal aliens. He concluded, however, that (p. 13):

> The push-pull notion is overly simplistic in that, among other things, it fails to take into account the fact that certain economic conditions have different effects depending on the attributes of migrants themselves.

Others have characterized the Mexico to U.S. labor stream as responding to both internal push forces and the pull of the U.S. economy (Alba, 1978). However, several studies indicate that the pull factors of the United States have the greatest importance in the case of the male Mexican immigrants.

Research by Houstoun (1983) and Waldinger (1984) has shown that male illegals typically come from the employed ranks of their home countries. Other studies indicate that the male illegal workers come to the United States with considerable work experience and are not from the most disadvantaged economic group in Mexico (Maram and Long, 1981; Mines and Nuckton, 1982; North and Houstoun, 1976; Reichert and Massey, 1979, 1980). In contrast, Zazueta and Corona (1979) found that a large proportion of illegal immigrant women had not had work experience in Mexico owing to lack of employment opportunities, and came to the United States seeking employment. So, it appears that both push and pull factors have an effect on Mexican immigrants, but males and females may respond to different factors.

Lee (1966) linked positive selectivity with pull factors and negative selectivity with push factors. While it is impossible to determine with certainty whether Mexican immigrants are responding to push or pull factors, or both, there is no indication of negative selectivity of Mexican immigrants. Alba (1978) reported that of a sample of immigrants at the El Paso and Laredo border points only 2 percent never had been in school and 65 percent had finished grade school. More than 50 percent had grown up in cities of more than 20,000 inhabitants and only 20 percent were farmers.

SELECTIVITY HYPOTHESES

Thus, it is hypothesized that the Mexican immigrant women in this study will be positively selected on a number of socioeconomic variables and furthermore, will have lower fertility than women who remained in Mexico.

Although there is often a lag time for women to alter their fertility behavior in response to the implementation of family planning programs or changes in development, it is obvious from Tables 4, 5, and 6 that women in Mexico altered their behavior very quickly once the decline began. Women who emigrated to the United States after 1975 would be expected to be affected by the changes in the fertility norms in Mexico, whereas women migrating prior to 1975 would not have been affected as greatly by these changes. Thus, women who immigrated since 1975 should have lower fertility (particularly lower current fertility) than women who immigrated prior to 1975. A discussion of the data and variables precedes the presentation of the results.

DATA AND VARIABLES

It is evident that a study of selectivity must compare the population of interest to the country of origin. In order to examine empirically the issue of selectivity, a sample of ever-married first-generation Mexican origin women in the United States is compared to a sample of ever-married women in Mexico. Data for the U.S. sample are from the 1980 Census Public Use Microfile Sample (PUMS-A) and the Mexican data are from the 1976-77 Mexican World Fertility Survey (EMS). Although the data were collected three to four years apart, the Mexican World Fertility Survey is an excellent source for such a comparison since it is individual-level data and contains many comparable variables.[4] A caveat for this comparison is that it is assumed that women in the Mexican sample are non-emigrants, although some may become migrants in the future. Furthermore, the United States census data do not have information on an immigrants's area or city of origin in Mexico, so direct matches of immigrants to their area of residence in Mexico are not possible.

An attempt was made to measure the variables in as similar a fashion as possible in the two samples. The primary variables of interest are the two fertility variables: children ever born and own children under age five.[5] The two main socioeconomic variables used in this analysis are education and labor force participation.

Education is measured as the number of years of completed schooling in the United States and is coded by educational levels in Mexico as follows:[6]

1) No education (never attended school)
2) Incomplete primary (<6 years)
3) Complete primary (6 years)
4) Incomplete secondary (7 or 8 years)
5) Complete secondary (9 years)
6) Incomplete preparatory or vocational (10 years)

88

7) Complete preparatory or vocational
       (11 or 12 years)
8) University or postgraduate
       (>12 years)

Employment experience in the United States
sample includes persons who reported that they
had worked in the week preceding the census;
persons who were unemployed or in the labor
reserve were included if they had worked since
1975. A woman was included in the labor force
in Mexico if she reported that she was working
at the time of the survey.

EVIDENCE OF SELECTIVITY

The results of the comparison of mean
values of the primary independent and dependent
variables are shown in Table 9 for Mexican women
by urban and rural status and for first-
generation Mexican origin women in the United
States.[7] The current fertility measure used for
this portion of the analysis is children under
five because it was the only measure of current
fertility available in the Mexican World
Fertility Survey. As was noted previously in
Tables 6 and 7, it is evident that fertility
levels in Mexico vary between urban and rural
areas, and vary among the states. Therefore,
the mean values in Table 9 are presented
separately for rural and urban women in Mexico.
Because we do not know specifically where the
immigrants came from in Mexico, this urban/rural
distinction is provided as a within Mexico
comparison, rather than a specific comparison of
immigrants to either rural or urban women.
It is evident that immigrant women are
positively selected on the socioeconomic
variables. This is especially true of
education, and will be discussed at length in
Chapter Eight. Of particular interest to the
question of push/pull factors is the labor force
participation variable. Again it should be
noted that this variable is not measured

identically in the two samples, but the differences in the means are dramatic in all age groups. The labor force participation rate is lowest for rural Mexican women, with urban Mexican women having higher participation levels; the United States levels are double and in some cases triple the Mexican rates. This indicates that employment in the U.S. exerts a pull and the lack of opportunities in Mexico may exert an additional push force.

Mexican mean fertility levels are considerably higher than those of first-generation Mexican women in the United States as seen in Figure 8 and Table 9. In the oldest age group (40-44), rural Mexican women had 3.6 more children ever born than the first-generation women in the United States, and urban women had 2.1 more children. What is of considerable interest is that current fertility, as measured by children under five, was nearly twice as high for rural Mexican women in every age group as that of the immigrants, and urban Mexican women had substantially higher rates as well. (See Figure 9.) This pattern indicates that in the period of rapidly decreasing fertility rates in Mexico (1972-77 are the reference dates for this survey), current fertility remained high in Mexico, but immigrant women had much lower current fertility than nonmigrants. It appears that the youngest women (15-19 and 20-24) in both the urban and rural areas of Mexico were the ones who had adopted the lower fertility norms, as seen in both fertility measures.

EVIDENCE OF FERTILITY DECLINES AMONG RECENT IMMIGRANTS

An examination of the mean number of children under five and children ever born indicates the effect of timing changes of fertility levels, as well as compositional differences in the immigrants coming to the United States over time. Timing of immigrations is likely to be another factor. As seen in

90

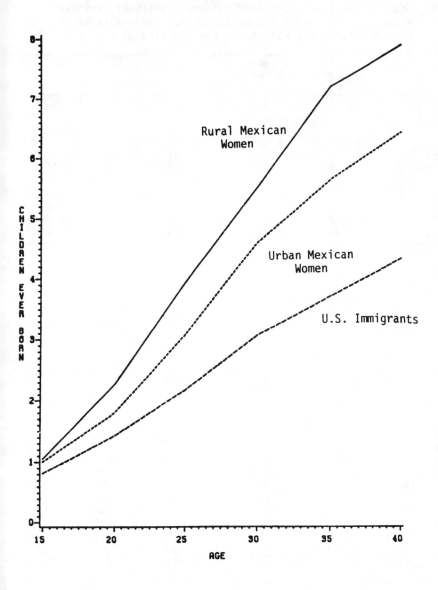

Figure 8. Children Ever Born for Urban and Rural Mexican Women
and First-Generation Mexican Women in the U.S.: 1977
and 1980

TABLE 9. Mean Values for a Number of Selected Variables, Mexican
Women by Urban and Rural Residence and Immigrants to the
United States, Six Cohorts of Ever-Married Women: 1977, 1980

	Children Ever Born	Children Under 5	Education	LFP*	(N)
15-19					
Mexico					
Rural	1.052	1.024	2.925	.071	252
Urban**	1.005	.995	4.991	.114	219
United States	.816	.664	7.867	.453	476
20-24					
Mexico					
Rural	2.272	1.765	3.318	.121	456
Urban	1.803	1.515	5.566	.181	664
United States	1.430	1.098	7.873	.598	1998
25-29					
Mexico					
Rural	3.940	1.904	2.694	.118	467
Urban	3.079	1.571	5.493	.227	735
United States	2.176	.983	7.832	.664	2594
30-34					
Mexico					
Rural	5.522	1.741	2.333	.167	402
Urban	4.605	1.315	4.556	.257	645
United States	3.070	.798	7.870	.628	2436
35-39					
Mexico					
Rural	7.212	1.531	1.841	.237	435
Urban	5.655	.925	4.451	.296	560
United States	3.716	.467	7.180	.667	1870
40-44					
Mexico					
Rural	7.911	.829	1.489	.213	315
Urban	6.444	.550	3.653	.262	455
United States	4.341	.199	6.602	.635	1680

* See text for definition of labor force participation, and how it
  differs between the two countries.

**Urban is defined as persons living in a city of 2,500 or more
  inhabitants.

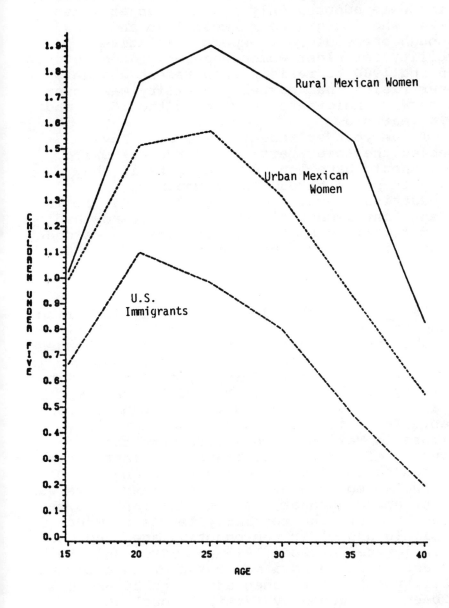

Figure 9. Children Under Five for Urban and Rural Mexican Women and First-Generation Mexican Women in the U.S.: 1977 and 1980

Table 10, it is apparent that the lower norms of Mexico were adopted only by the younger women (15-24) who immigrated between 1975 and 1980. Although one would not expect cumulative fertility for older women who immigrated between 1975 and 1980 to reflect such recent changes, it is surprising that current fertility was lower for recent immigrants only among the 15-24 and 30-34 year olds.

These younger recent immigrants have accepted the lower fertility norms of Mexico, which should have long-term effects if they remain in place throughout a woman's reproductive years. From ages 25 to 44, it is evident that recent migrant women already had higher fertility than prior immigrants, as seen in the children ever born measure.

SUMMARY

Fertility declined precipitously in Mexico during the 1970s largely as a result of the availability of family planning. These changes uniformly reached women of different ages and in all geographic areas. However, differences in fertility levels continue to exist when comparing certain groups such as urban and rural women. There is little doubt that fertility declines in Mexico in the 1970s were the beginning of a fertility transition that can be expected to continue into the 1980s and beyond.

The acceptance of lower fertility norms was evident among younger, recent immigrants to the United States. The fertility levels of women in the middle and older reproductive ages and who had immigrated between 1975 and 1980 indicate that assimilation is a major factor in altering fertility norms for women after age 25 and has not been confounded by fertility declines in Mexico. It is not evident what effect the fertility declines in Mexico will have for immigrants during the coming years. Clearly there will be a movement toward convergence of fertility levels between the two countries,

TABLE 10. Mean Number of Children Under Five and Children Ever Born
for Recent and Previous Mexican Immigrant Women,
Six Cohorts of Ever-Married Women: 1980

First Generation Immigrant Groups	AGE GROUPS					
	15-19	20-24	25-29	30-34	35-39	40-44
A. CHILDREN UNDER FIVE						
1975-1980	.579	1.011	1.031	.796	.598	.222
Prior to 1975	.795	1.180	.964	.799	.443	.196
B. CHILDREN EVER BORN						
1975-1980	.755	1.323	2.199	3.120	4.070	5.280
Prior to 1975	.910	1.531	2.166	3.056	3.651	4.189

although it is likely that Mexican fertility
will remain substantially higher than that of
the United States.   It can be expected that,
with time, acceptance of the lower fertility
norms will be seen in the middle and older
reproductive ages of both Mexican women and
immigrants to the U.S.

There is strong evidence of positive
selectivity of female Mexican immigrants based
on educational attainment and labor force
participation.   Furthermore, the immigrant women
have lower current and cumulative fertility than
women remaining in Mexico.   It is unfortunate a
direct comparison of immigrant women to women
from their specific origin in Mexico cannot be
made, but it is apparent that immigration is
selective of both rural and urban Mexican women.
It is evident that women in the youngest ages
accepted the lower fertility norms and that
there is strong evidence of selectivity of
Mexican immigrants to the U.S.   Although
fertility declined in Mexico during the 1970s,
it did not mask or confound the selectivity
effect.   A comparison of recent immigrants to
other Mexican immigrants also indicates strong
evidence of assimilation, which will be explored
in detail in the next chapter.

CHAPTER 7

DISRUPTION AND ASSIMILATION

In this chapter the effects of disruption and assimilation on the fertility of Mexican origin women are examined using data from the 1970 and 1980 U.S. Censuses. One of the research hypotheses for this portion of the analysis predicts that disruption lowers fertility for first-generation women. This should be most evident in the current fertility measure around the time of the actual migration, but the effect is likely to persist throughout the childbearing years when other socioeconomic and demographic variables are controlled. A second hypothesis is that Mexican immigrant women come closer to the fertility behavior of women in the United States as time living in the U.S. increases. Evidence of assimilation should be evident among the native-born women through its depressing effect on both current and cumulative fertility. These two hypotheses are considered to be complementary, rather than competing hypotheses in that they predict the behavior of two separate groups of Mexican origin women.

Descriptive statistics are presented first. Next, regression results are analyzed separately for 1970 and 1980, followed by an analysis of changes from 1970 to 1980. Although data on three generations were included in the 1970 U.S. Census, only information for the first-generation and the second-or higher-generation will be presented here in order to provide comparable statistics for 1970 with 1980. (See Bean et al., 1984, for detailed statistics on the three Mexican origin generations in 1970.)

VARIABLES

The dependent variables utilized in this analysis are children under three and children ever born. The independent variables are: age,

97

education, rural/urban residence, marital disruption, region, employment experience, and family income. (See Table 11.) Region is introduced here as a dummy variable delineating the five southwestern states (Arizona, California, Colorado, New Mexico, and Texas) from all other states. This variable controls for the differences in spatial distribution of the two generational groups. The vast majority of Mexican immigrants initially reside in the Southwest; native-born Mexican immigrants are more likely to migrate to other places within the United States. Urban population is defined as all persons living in urbanized areas and in places of 2,500 or more inhabitants outside urbanized areas.[1]

The definition of employment experience changed slightly from 1970 to 1980. In both Censuses, employment experience was asked of all persons 16 years or age and over in the civilian labor force. Employed persons reported the occupation at which they had worked the most hours in the week preceding the census. In 1970, the experienced unemployed and persons in the labor reserve reported their last occupation, unless their previous employment was prior to 1960. In 1980, occupation was defined as the kind of work the person was doing at a job or business if employed since 1975. The primary difference in the definition between the two Censuses is the definition of labor reserve. In 1970, it was defined as experienced workers who were not in the labor force at the time of the census, but who had worked between 1960 and 1970. In 1980, the labor reserve was limited to those who had worked since 1975.

DESCRIPTIVE STATISTICS

The means and standard deviations of the independent and dependent variables are shown in Tables 12 (1970) and 13 (1980) by age group. The mean number of children ever born declined in ages 20-39 between 1970 and 1980, but rose

Table 11. Description of Independent and Dependent Variables

Variable	Abbreviation	Measurement
Children ever born	CEB	Number of children ever born to woman
Children under three	Children <3	Number of children under age three allocated to woman
Age	Age	Respondent's age in years at time of the census
Education	Educ	Completed years of schooling
Rural/urban residence	Rural	Dummy variable: 0=Urban 1=Rural
Marital Disruption	Disrupt	Dummy variable:0=Never disrupted 1=Disrupted
Region	SW	Dummy variable: 0=not a south-western state 1=AZ, CA, CO, NM, or TX
Employment experience	LFP	Dummy Variable: 0=did not work 5 years prior to Census 1=did work 5 years prior to Census
Family income	Faminc	Income of all family members In 1970: in 1,000s of dollars In 1980: in dollars
First generation	Gen1	Dummy variable: 0=not first generation Mexican origin 1=first genera-tion Mexican origin
Native born	Gen2	Dummy variable: 0=not native born Mexican origin 1=native-born of Mexican origin

Table 12. Means and Standard Deviations of Variables, Ever-Married Mexican Origin and Non-Spanish Origin White Women, Ages 15-44: 1970

AGE GROUPS

Variable	15-19 Mean	15-19 S.D.	20-24 Mean	20-24 S.D.	25-29 Mean	25-29 S.D.	30-34 Mean	30-34 S.D.	35-39 Mean	35-39 S.D.	40-44 Mean	40-44 S.D.
CEB	.68	.81	1.20	1.17	2.10	1.53	3.07	1.90	3.54	2.27	3.47	2.38
Children <3	.53	.68	.63	.69	.54	.65	.32	.56	.17	.44	.08	.30
Age	17.00	1.11	22.20	1.34	26.97	1.38	31.98	1.44	37.06	1.41	41.98	1.41
Educ	10.37	2.30	11.53	2.62	11.55	3.02	10.99	3.22	10.61	3.49	10.33	3.62
Rural	.25	.43	.22	.41	.23	.42	.22	.41	.23	.42	.24	.43
Disrupt	.07	.25	.09	.28	.09	.29	.10	.29	.11	.31	.12	.32
Sw	.53	.50	.48	.50	.47	.50	.50	.50	.48	.50	.45	.50
LFP	.64	.48	.83	.37	.82	.39	.70	.46	.67	.47	.66	.48
Faminc	8.14	12.35	9.23	9.86	10.64	10.51	11.20	10.70	11.93	10.98	12.38	10.72
Gen1	.05	.21	.06	.23	.07	.25	.08	.28	.08	.28	.07	.25
Gen2	.53	.50	.45	.50	.42	.49	.42	.49	.40	.49	.36	.48
N	1176		4421		5050		4485		4272		4351	

100

Table 13. Means and Standard Deviations of Variables, Ever-Married Mexican Origin and Non-Spanish Origin White Women, Ages 15-44: 1980

	AGE GROUPS											
	15-19		20-24		25-29		30-34		35-39		40-44	
Variable	Mean	S.D.	Mean	S.D.	Mean	S.D.	Mean	S.D.	Mean	S.D.	Mean	S.D.
CEB	.71	.78	1.15	1.04	1.68	1.31	2.35	1.54	2.93	1.84	3.50	2.18
Children <3	.56	.73	.59	.67	.46	.61	.30	.52	.13	.37	.04	.21
Age	18.10	1.07	22.28	1.37	27.02	1.42	31.93	1.39	36.89	1.39	41.92	1.39
Educ	10.29	2.56	10.94	2.94	11.48	3.48	11.55	3.61	11.25	3.70	10.60	3.83
Rural	.07	.26	.08	.27	.08	.28	.10	.29	.12	.32	.12	.33
Disrupt	.08	.27	.13	.33	.14	.35	.16	.36	.17	.37	.18	.39
Sw	.67	.47	.59	.49	.56	.50	.52	.50	.48	.50	.50	.50
LFP	.67	.47	.81	.39	.79	.41	.76	.43	.73	.45	.72	.44
Faminc	14387	11659	15554	10838	18158	11773	20277	13669	22257	14841	24904	144683
Gen1	.19	.39	.20	.40	.19	.39	.19	.39	.18	.38	.19	.39
Gen2	.52	.50	.41	.49	.36	.48	.32	.47	.29	.45	.30	.46
N	2,503		10,001		13,650		13,157		10,440		8,734	

101

slightly from 3.47 to 3.50 children in the oldest age group, and from .68 to .71 in the 15-19 age group. In all ages there was substantial variation around the mean for both fertility measures. Educational levels rose in 1980 for the three oldest age groups, perhaps indicating postponement of marriage among women with higher levels of education. The slight declines in educational attainment in the three youngest age groups may be an indication of the large increase in the proportion of first-generation women who may have been educated at least partially in Mexico. The proportion of women living in rural areas decreased markedly from 1970 to 1980; this may be a result of the coding of urban in the 1980 sample. (See Footnote 1 to this chapter.) The proportion of women living in the Southwest increased from 1970 to 1980. Perhaps one of the most striking findings in a comparison of Tables 12 and 13 is the dramatic increase in the proportion of first-generation women in every age, which is a result of improved census coverage in 1980 and the large influx of legal and illegal immigrants during the 1970s. This can be expected to have a major impact on fertility levels and trends.

Descriptive statistics for two generations of the Mexican origin population and non-Spanish origin whites by five-year age group are shown in Table 14 for 1970 and Table 15 for 1980. These tables include statistics for education and the two dependent variables, as these are the main variables of interest. These two tables provide initial support for the assimilation hypothesis in that in both 1970 and 1980 mean values of cumulative and current fertility within each age group consistently decline moving from first-generation to native-born to non-Spanish origin white women.

Another finding from Tables 14 and 15 are that mean levels of current and cumulative fertility decrease from 1970 to 1980 for both Mexican origin groups and non-Spanish origin whites. The only exception is that the mean

102

TABLE 14. Means for Selected Variables for Two Generational Groups of Mexican Origin and Non-Spanish Origin Whites, Six Cohorts of Ever-Married Women: 1970

	AGE GROUPS					
	15-19	20-24	25-29	30-34	35-39	40-44
A. FIRST GENERATION						
CEB	.930	1.538	2..487	3.622	4.329	4.668
Children < 3	.684	.771	.727	.460	.283	.206
Education	7.315	7.988	7.728	6.918	6.288	5.852
N	57	249	351	378	353	301
B. NATIVE BORN						
CEB	.771	1.370	2.356	3.364	4.046	4.075
Children < 3	.598	.699	.558	.349	.201	.105
Education	10.187	11.104	10.876	10.338	9.737	8.991
N	619	1981	2099	1864	1709	1570
C. NON-SPANISH ORIGIN WHITES						
CEB	.534	1.000	1.850	2.740	3.016	2.943
Children < 3	.418	.560	.510	.280	.137	.047
Education	10.952	12.272	12.422	12.086	12.005	11.608
N	500	2191	2600	2243	2210	2480

TABLE 15. Means of Selected Variables for Two Generational Groups
of Mexican Origin and Non-Spanish Origin Whites, Six
Cohorts of Ever-Married Women: 1980

	AGE GROUPS					
	15-19	20-24	25-29	30-34	35-39	40-44

A. FIRST GENERATION						
CEB	.816	1.430	2.176	3.070	3.716	4.341
Children < 3	.612	.736	.551	.422	.241	.096
Education	7.867	7.873	7.832	7.870	7.180	6.602
N	478	1998	2594	2436	1870	1680

B. NATIVE BORN						
CEB	.761	1.307	1.916	2.660	3.452	4.037
Children < 3	.624	.642	.466	.295	.144	.042
Education	10.716	11.121	11.194	10.930	10.323	9.782
N	1314	4065	4979	4270	3030	2585

C.NON-SPANISH ORIGIN WHITES						
CEB	.534	.844	1.283	1.874	2.384	2.870
Children < 3	.412	.452	.420	.256	.086	.020
Education	11.137	12.192	12.730	12.643	12.411	12.114
N	712	3938	6078	6451	5540	4469

104

number of children ever born remained constant
for the 15-19 year old non-Spanish origin white
women. These results indicate that both the
pace and overall levels of fertility have
diminished over the decade for all three groups.
    These patterns may be seen even more
clearly in Figures 10-13. Mean values of
children ever born by age group of mother are
shown in Figure 10 for 1970 and Figure 11 for
1980. From these two figures it is evident that
the divergence between the two Mexican
populations from other whites begins before ages
20-24 and becomes most pronounced in the oldest
reproductive ages. There are some aberrations
in the 1970 data that cannot be explained;
specifically, the mean number of children ever
born decreases from ages 35-39 to 40-44 for both
native-born and non-Spanish origin white women.
    Means for children under three are shown in
Figure 12 for 1970 and Figure 13 for 1980. The
expected pattern of highest current fertility
for first-generation women is evident in both
figures, with the exception of women ages 15-19
in 1980. The native-born women have patterns
fairly close with those of non-Spanish origin
whites in 1980, particularly after age 25. This
may be indicative of greater assimilation of the
second generation in 1980.
    The last variable of interest shown in
Tables 14 and 15 is education. The education
levels rose over the decade for all groups
except the 20-24 years olds in the first
generation. Educational attainment was about
three years less for first-generation than for
native-born Mexican Americans, and an additional
1.5 to 2 years below that of non-Spanish origin
whites. This reflects the larger proportion of
first-generation women in the 1980 sample who
received some, or all, of their education in
Mexico, where educational attainment is
universally lower than in the United States, as
observed in Chapter Six. The effect on
fertility of the country in which women received

105

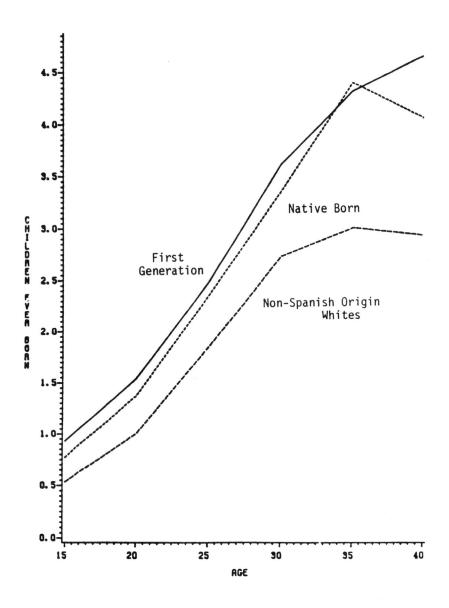

Figure 10.   Mean Number of Children Ever Born for Ever-Married
             Mexican Origin and Non-Spanish Origin White Women:
             1970

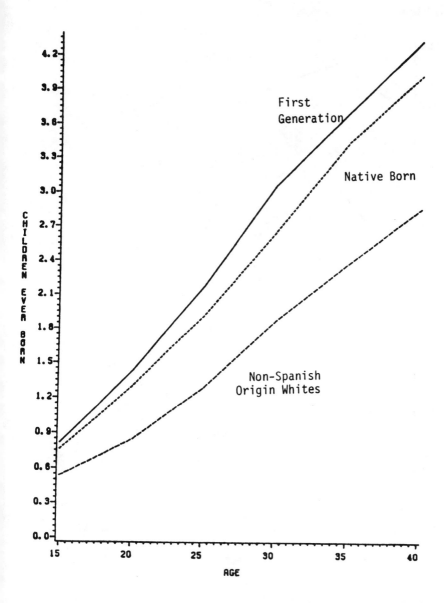

Figure 11. Mean Number of Children Ever Born for Ever-Married Mexican Origin and Non-Spanish Origin White Women: 1980

107

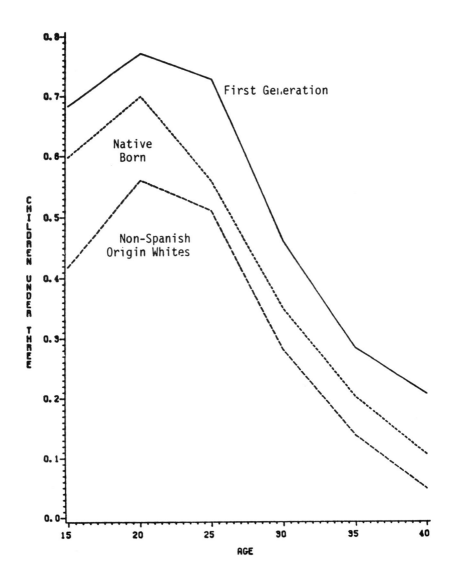

Figure 12.   Mean Number of Children Under Three for Ever-Married
Mexican Origin and Non-Spanish Origin White Women:
1970

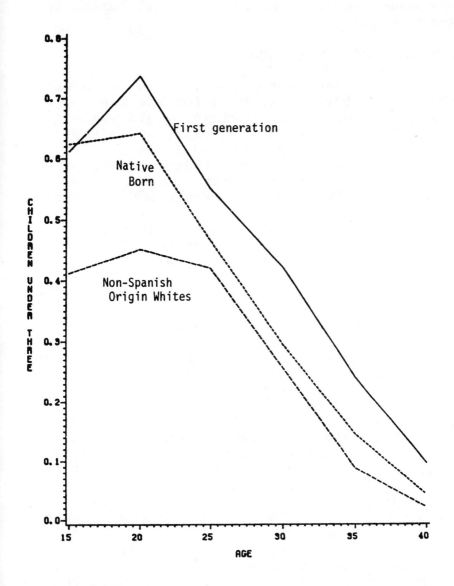

Figure 13.   Mean Number of Children Under Three for Ever-Married Mexican Origin and Non-Spanish Origin White Women: 1980

109

their education will be discussed at length in Chapter Eight.

GROSS AND NET DEVIATIONS

The gross and net deviations in the average number of children ever born for the two generational groups of Mexican origin women from those of non-Spanish origin white women are shown in Table 16 for 1970 and Table 17 for 1980. The gross deviations indicate average fertility deviations for that group from the mean value for non-Spanish origin women without controlling for the influence of any other variables. The net deviations reflect that group's deviation from the mean fertility of non-Spanish origin white women, after the controls have been included.

A series of regression models were computed to assess the influence of the control variables. Age was added first, then education, then the remaining control variables were included: female employment experience, region, family income, marital disruption dummy variable, and urban/rural residence. The addition of age had very little impact on fertility patterns; however, the addition of education resulted in dramatic changes. The fertility patterns in the full model did not change much from the model in which education was added, but are presented here with the realization that education is the primary variable accounting for the differences between the gross and net deviations.

Looking first at Table 16, the gross fertility deviations are significantly positive for both generations in every age group. The gross deviations are smaller for native-born women than for first-generation women in each age group, which supports the assimilation hypothesis. However, once the control variables are taken into account, cumulative fertility is lower among first-generation women than among non-Spanish origin whites from ages 20 to 34,

110

TABLE 16.   Gross and Net Deviations in Average Number of Children Ever
Born for Two Generational Groups of Mexican Women from
Non-Spanish Origin White Women, Six Cohorts of Ever-Married
Women: 1970

	AGE GROUPS					
	15-19	20-24	25-29	30-34	35-39	40-44
A. GROSS DEVIATIONS						
First Generation	.396*	.535*	.641*	.882*	1.312*	1.725*
Native Born	.237*	.367*	.509*	.624*	1.030*	1.132*
Constant	.534	1.002	1.847	2.740	3.016	2.943
R²	.025	.028	.030	.032	.057	.069
B. NET DEVIATIONS						
First Generation	.053	-.385*	-.375*	-.053	.290	.829*
Native Born	.154	.157*	.224*	.343*	.718*	.822*
Constant	-1.285	-1.139	-1.091	1.461	3.666	7.433
R²	.105	.250	.229	.145	.154	.154

*significant at p=.01

111

TABLE 17. Gross and Net Deviations in Average Number of Children Ever Born for Two Generational Groups of Mexican Women from Non-Spanish Origin White Women, Six Cohorts of Ever-Married Women: 1980

	AGE GROUPS					
	15-19	20-24	25-29	30-34	35-39	40-44

A. GROSS DEVIATIONS

	15-19	20-24	25-29	30-34	35-39	40-44
First Generation	.282*	.585*	.892*	1.196*	1.332*	1.470*
Native Born	.228*	.463*	.633*	.786*	1.068*	1.167*
Constant	.534	.844	1.283	1.874	2.384	2.870
R^2	.020	.058	.080	.101	.102	.089

B. NET DEVIATIONS

	15-19	20-24	25-29	30-34	35-39	40-44
First Generation	.037	.064	.307*	.293*	.503*	.498*
Native Born	.232*	.378*	.509*	.421*	.738*	.731*
Constant	-.311	-1.097	-.769	.364	-.771	-.304
R^2	.090	.214	.242	.238	.211	.170

*significant at p=.01

112

and is significantly lower than it is among non-
Spanish origin whites from ages 20 to 29. That
is, once the two generational groups of Mexican
origin women have the same education levels
statistically as that of non-Spanish origin
white women, a different fertility pattern
emerges. As observed in Table 9 (Chapter Six)
and Tables 14 and 15, education levels are much
lower among immigrant Mexican-origin women
compared to non-Spanish origin white women, even
though the immigrant women have high levels of
education as compared to non-immigrant women
remaining in Mexico. Thus, the fertility
patterns change dramatically once education is
controlled statistically. The children ever
born measure is significantly higher than that
of non-Spanish origin whites only in the oldest
age group of the first generation. This pattern
of lower fertility in the first generation
supports the disruption hypothesis; fertility is
lowered for a time surrounding the actual
immigration, but women in successive generations
are not affected.

The fertility deviations for native-born
women are all positive, and significant except
for the youngest age group (15-19) in 1970.
This pattern indicates that cumulative fertility
is already higher than that of non-Spanish
origin whites by ages 20-24 and that this higher
fertility remains above that of non-Spanish
origin whites throughout the childbearing years.
That is, high initial fertility is translated
into higher fertility than for non-Spanish
whites throughout the reproductive years.

In comparing the net deviations in Table 17
with Table 16, we can see that in 1980
cumulative fertility is significant within each
age group in the first generation except in the
two youngest age groups. As opposed to 1970,
there are no age groups in 1980 for which
cumulative fertility is negative for the first
generation. However, cumulative fertility did
remain lower for the first generation than that
of the native-born women, again indicating the

effect of disruption on fertility of first-generation women.

Deviations in current fertility are shown in Tables 18 (1970) and 19 (1980). Looking first at Table 18, again all the gross fertility deviations are positive and significant. The current fertility deviations for the first-generation are substantially higher than those of the native-born women, once again providing support for the assimilation hypothesis. With the addition of the controls, current fertility in the first generation is significantly higher only after ages 25-29, and is even lower than that of non-Spanish origin whites in the 20-24 age group. Current fertility for the native-born women is not significantly different at ages 15-19 and 25-29. Comparing Tables 18 and 19, the gross deviations in 1980 are similar to the patterns exhibited in 1970 in that all the gross fertility measures deviate significantly and positively from non-Spanish origin whites. In both 1970 and 1980, current fertility is not significantly different from that of non-Spanish origin whites for the 25-29 year old native-born women. In 1980, current fertility of native-born women is actually lower than that of non-Spanish origin white women in the 30-34 age group. This indicates that current fertility levels of native-born women are approaching those of non-Spanish origin white women during the middle childbearing years, deviating only at the youngest and oldest childbearing years. That is, native-born women begin their childbearing earlier and continue it longer than non-Spanish origin women, as seen in the children ever born measure. However, the pace of childbearing for native-born women is similar to that of non-Spanish origin whites, lending support to the assimilation hypothesis.

By looking at Tables 16 and 18 as a pair, and Tables 17 and 19, we see that these results support the research hypotheses. The pattern of gross deviations in the case of each of the fertility measures supports the assimilation

114

TABLE 18. Gross and Net Deviations in Average Number of Children Under Three for Two Generational Groups of Mexican Women from Non-Spanish Origin White Women, Six Cohorts of Ever-Married Women: 1970

| | AGE GROUPS | | | | | |
	15-19	20-24	25-29	30-34	35-39	40-44
	A. GROSS DEVIATIONS					
First Generation	.266*	.217*	.218*	.181*	.147*	.159*
Native Born	.180*	.145*	.050*	.070*	.064*	.058*
Constant	.418	.554	.508	.279	.137	.468
R^2	.019	.013	.007	.009	.013	.022
	B. NET DEVIATIONS					
First Generation	.039	-.027	.172*	.143*	.124*	.129*
Native Born	.124	.080*	.033	.061*	.072*	.042*
Constant	-.917	.967	1.433	1.615	.960	.721
R^2	.072	.059	.035	.027	.026	.039

*significant at p=.01

115

TABLE 19. Gross and Net Deviations in Average Number of Children Under Three for Two Generational Groups of Mexican Women from Non-Spanish Origin White Women, Six Cohorts of Ever-Married Women: 1980

	AGE GROUPS					
	15-19	20-24	25-29	30-34	35-39	40-44

A. GROSS DEVIATIONS

	15-19	20-24	25-29	30-34	35-39	40-44
First Generation	.120*	.284*	.131*	.166*	.156*	.076*
Native Born	.212*	.190*	.047*	.039*	.059*	.022*
Constant	.412	.452	.419	.256	.086	.020
R^2	.017	.028	.006	.014	.025	.018

B. NET DEVIATIONS

	15-19	20-24	25-29	30-34	35-39	40-44
First Generation	.052	.104*	.060*	.103*	.097*	.079*
Native Born	.205*	.164*	.038	-.003	.024	.026*
Constant	.235	.800	1.129	1.458	1.180	.267
R^2	.045	.084	.052	.050	.052	.028

*significant at p=.01

116

hypothesis. Furthermore, the pattern of net
deviations of the number of children under three
supports the assimilation hypothesis among the
native-born women, with the exception of the two
youngest age groups. The effects of disruption
are apparent, primarily in the net deviations of
the children ever born measure. There is some
indication of a short-term effect in the younger
ages, which most likely occurs near the time of
the actual immigration. The long-term effects
of disruption are more evident in 1970 in the
deviations of the children ever born measure.
In 1980, a more heterogeneous population may be
masking the long-term disruption effect. This
proposition will be examined in more detail in
Chapter Eight.
     It is obvious that disaggregating the
Mexican origin population by generational status
and age merely provides an initial step in
determining the effects of immigration on
fertility. Another way of examining this issue
is to consider the long-term effects of
immigration on fertility of specific age
cohorts. In an examination of age cohorts it is
possible to discern in what manner disruption
and immigration affect fertility over time for a
cohort, rather than masking inferences about
time from cross-sectional data. We now turn to
this discussion.

LIFE-COURSE EFFECTS OF ASSIMILATION AND
DISRUPTION

     For an analysis of how migration depresses
fertility over the lifetime of a migrant, it
would be preferable to have information on real
cohorts at several time points, but this study
is limited by having only two time points and
synthetic cohorts. Nevertheless, this provides
for more detail on the life course of immigrants
than do cross-sectional data. The net
deviations of the two generational groups of
Mexican origin women from non-Spanish origin
whites as measured by the average number of

children under three and children ever born are
shown in Table 20 for four age cohorts. The
first two cohorts of first-generation women had
low current fertility in 1970, but by 1980 their
current fertility was significantly higher than
for non-Spanish origin whites. Assuming that
immigration is concentrated in the late teens
and early twenties, this pattern is indicative
of current fertility being depressed around the
time of the migration, then fertility being
"made-up" after the migration, reaching a peak
5-10 years following the migration. The
deviation in current fertility for the third and
fourth cohorts of native-born women remained
significantly positive from 1970 to 1980,
although the magnitude decreased in 1980 as an
indication of the cohort's advancement in the
reproductive years and possibly some
assimilation if they have been in the United
States for some time.

The life-course patterns of current
fertility are not as obvious among the native-
born Mexican origin women. The first and third
cohorts had positive, but not significant,
deviations in both 1970 and 1980, while the
fourth cohort had significant deviations in both
years. The second cohort had a significantly
positive deviation by 1970, but by 1980, the
deviation was negative and non-significant.
This may be indicative of sub-cultural forces
operating at certain ages as described by St.
John and Grasmick (1985).

Life-course events are more evident when
looking at the children ever born measure. The
second, third, and fourth cohorts of the first-
generation all had negative deviations from non-
Spanish origin whites in 1970. By 1980 they all
had significantly positive deviations and to
some degree had made-up their previously lost
fertility. The pattern for children ever born
for the native-born women was fairly similar to
that of the first generation. The magnitude of
the fertility deviations increased from 1970 to
1980 across all age cohorts and was significant

118

TABLE 20. COHORT COMPARISON OF NET DEVIATIONS[a] IN AVERAGE NUMBER OF CHILDREN UNDER THREE AND CHILDREN EVER BORN FOR TWO GENERATIONAL GROUPS OF MEXICAN ORIGIN WOMEN FROM NON-SPANISH ORIGIN WHITE WOMEN, FOUR COHORTS OF EVER-MARRIED WOMEN, 1970 TO 1980.

	COHORT I		COHORT II		COHORT III		COHORT IV	
	15-19 In 1970	25-29 In 1980	20-24 In 1970	30-34 In 1980	25-29 In 1970	35-39 In 1980	30-34 In 1970	40-44 In 1980
A. Children Under Three								
First Generation	.039	.060*	-.027	.103*	.172*	.097*	.143*	.079*
Native Born	.124	.038	.080*	-.003	.033	.024	.061*	.026*
B. Children Ever Born								
First Generation	.053	.307*	-.385*	.293*	-.375*	.503*	-.053	.498*
Native Born	.154	.509*	.157*	.421*	.224*	.738*	.343*	.731*
N	1,176	13,650	4,421	13,157	5,050	10,440	4,485	8,734

[a] Net of: age, education, marital status, region, urban/rural residence, family income, and employment experience.

* Significant at p = .01.

119

in every cohort except the 15-19 year olds in 1970. These results are strongly indicative again of a disruption effect in the first generation. Although cumulative fertility is made-up somewhat in the decade, fertility levels for the first generation deviate less from non-Spanish origin whites than do those of native-born women.

In summary, the cohort/life-cycle analysis supports the earlier cross-sectional results of both a disruptive effect on the fertility of Mexican immigrant women and an assimilation effect among the native-born Mexican women. The cohort approach further illuminates a pattern that is not as obvious in the cross-sectional data. While there is a short-term disruption effect, it appears that the long-term effects are muted because women later make-up their lost fertility to some degree. Although the net fertility deviations of children ever born are lower for immigrant women than for native-born Mexican origin women, there is clear evidence of assimilation among all of the cohorts in 1980 when examining the current fertility measure. Thus, we again have evidence supporting both disruption (in the first-generation) and assimilation (among the native-born women).

SUMMARY

In this chapter, we have found support for the assimilation hypothesis by examining mean numbers of children ever born and children under three. Examined separately by age groups, the mean fertility measures decline consistently across first-generation Mexican origin, native-born Mexican American, and non-Spanish origin women. The regression results for the gross deviations in fertility between the two generational groups and non-Spanish origin women also provide evidence of assimilation. However, once control variables--particularly education--have been included in the regression equation, a different pattern emerges. Fertility is lower

120

in the first generation than it is among native-born women, and in some cases, lower than it is among non-Spanish origin whites. Long-term and short-term disruptive effects are evident in both 1970 and 1980, although the effects are most obvious in 1970. In a cohort analysis, only the short-term effects of disruption are apparent. That is, fertility appears to be depressed around the time of the actual immigration, but Mexican immigrant women later make-up their postponed or delayed childbearing. Assimilation was evident in the children under three measure for all four cohorts.

In the following chapter two issues that have been addressed briefly in this and previous chapters are examined. It appears that there may be other factors that either enhance or confound the effects of assimilation and disruption. Two of these factors that deserve a more thorough examination are the effects of country of education and the possible legal status of the immigrant.

CHAPTER 8

COMPOSITIONAL FACTORS AND THE EFFECTS OF IMMIGRATION ON FERTILITY

The fertility patterns of the first-generation Mexican origin population according to immigrant status and country of education are examined in this chapter. This analysis is undertaken because the composition of the first generation in the 1980 Census is different from that of previous censuses. This is primarily because of the large number of undocumenteds included in the 1980 Census (Warren and Passel, 1987). Also, it is likely that the effects of immigration on fertility (selectivity, disruption, and assimilation) that have been examined in detail in earlier chapters operate differently in various subpopulations. Thus, it is important to study the separate effects of selectivity, disruption, and assimilation for self-reported naturalized citizens and for groups that consist of large numbers of legal and illegal immigrants.

Furthermore, the country of education is a key variable among women in the first generation. Because education generally has an inverse relationship with fertility (Cho, Grabill, and Bogue, 1970; Rindfuss and Sweet, 1977; Westoff and Ryder, 1977), it is expected that women educated in a country such as the United States have greater access to education and should have lower fertility. As seen in Table 10 of Chapter 6, it is evident that years of schooling is much higher for ever-married women in the United States than for women in Mexico. Information on country of education is not available from U.S. census data. However, by using information on age of the woman at the time of the census, five-year intervals of date of arrival into the United States, and amount of education, it is possible to approximate the likely country of a woman's education: Mexico, the United States, or a mixture of both. In

this chapter, fertility as it varies by
immigrant status is discussed, followed by an
analysis of fertility according to country of
education.

HYPOTHESIZED RELATIONSHIPS

To study the effect of immigrant status on
fertility, it is necessary to distinguish among
the possible immigrant categories. In the 1980
Census, citizenship status was a self-reported
item, so it is possible to identify members of
that group. However it is not possible to
distinguish illegal from legal immigrants using
the 1980 Census data. Therefore, this analysis
draws on a trichotomy of the first generation
based on other census data, used by Bean,
Browning, and Frisbie (1984), which was
described earlier in Chapter 4. This
categorization is as follows:

1) Category I: post-1975 immigrants
who are Mexican born
and not citizens of the
U.S.

2) Category II: pre-1975 immigrants who
are Mexican born and
not citizens of the
U.S.

3) Category III: Mexican born persons
who self-report that
they are U.S.
naturalized citizens

As Bean, Browning, and Frisbie reported, there
is some overlap in each of these categories.
Based on an analysis by Warren and Passel
(1987), Category I contains about two-thirds
illegals. It is estimated that 35 percent
actually have achieved citizenship status in
Category III. These categories are utilized for
the present analysis to indicate patterns of
fertility associated with the three groups

rather than to determine the legality of specific individuals.

As discussed in Chapter 4, it is likely that selectivity, disruption, and assimilation affect the heterogeneous first-generation population differently. Because we are making comparisons within the first generation in this analysis and don't make any comparisons with Mexican women, it is not possible to address the issue of selectivity directly. Instead, this portion of the analysis will focus on disruption and assimilation. Disruption is expected to be evident particularly in the case of Category I women because they are the most recent migrants and may contain a large proportion of illegals. Based on Browning and Cullen's findings (1983), it is evident that there is frequent circular migration between Mexico and the United States. Opitz and Frisbie (1985) have shown that eight times as many recent male immigrants are married with spouse absent than the remainder of the male Mexican origin population. Disruption should be evident in lower current fertility among recent immigrants. Because we are looking at immigrants who came to the U.S. between 1975 an1 1980 in Category I, it is not possible to de ermine the long-term effects of disruption on cu lative fertility for this group.

Assimilation should have large effects on the fertility of women in Categories II and III, but particularly in Category III, as many of these women already have taken steps to become U.S. citizens. It may be difficult to distinguish precisely the effects of assimilation and disruption because they are intertwined to some degree and because the immigrant status categories overlap, but some patterns should be apparent.

RESULTS

Mean values of children under age three, children ever born, and education are provided in Table 21 for the three immigrant categories

124

Table 21. Means for Selected Variables for Post-1975 and Pre-1975
Immigrant Women, Self-reported Naturalized Citizens, and
Native-born Mexican Origin Women, Six Cohorts of Ever-
Married Women, United States: 1980

Variable			Age groups			
	15-19	20-24	25-29	30-34	35-39	40-44
Post-1975 Immigrants						
CEB	.76	1.34	2.18	3.06	4.01	5.31
Children < 3	.55	.73	.60	.44	.27	.10
Education	6.89	6.85	6.45	7.21	5.88	6.15
N	275	876	670	474	251	209
Pre-1975 Immigrants						
CEB	.95	1.61	2.16	3.12	3.80	4.49
Children < 3	.78	.78	.54	.43	.26	.11
Education	9.33	8.40	7.71	7.89	7.13	6.04
N	121	748	1360	1478	1078	974
Naturalized Citizens						
CEB	.81	1.29	2.20	2.95	3.41	3.65
Children < 3	.58	.66	.53	.38	.19	.07
Education	8.98	9.22	9.74	8.45	7.96	7.90
N	83	374	565	484	542	498
Native Born						
CEB	.76	1.31	1.92	2.66	3.45	4.04
Children < 3	.62	.64	.47	.30	.14	.04
Education	10.72	11.12	11.19	10.93	10.32	9.78
N	1314	4065	4979	4270	3030	2585

125

by five-year age groups. The only definitive
pattern is that among the immigrants, education
is highest for naturalized citizens, except for
the 15-19 year olds; in that age group, pre-1975
immigrants had the highest educational levels.
The number of children under age three is
highest for post-1975 immigrants between ages 25
and 39, but the pre-1975 immigrants had the
highest number of children under age three in
the other three age groups. The mean number of
children ever born is highest for post-1975
immigrants only in the two oldest age groups
(35-39 and 40-44); it is highest for naturalized
citizens in the 25-29 age group, although the
between group differences are negligible for
that age group.

Regression results are presented in Tables
22 and 23. Again, the gross deviations indicate
the average fertility deviation of each group
from non-Spanish origin white women without
controlling for the influence of any other
variables. The net deviations control for the
effects of age, education, marital status,
urban/rural residence, family income, and
employment experience. The coefficients for the
native-born women are shown in Tables 22 and 23
because they were included in the regression
equations. However, because this analysis
focuses on the first generation, the native-born
group will not be discussed in this section.

It can be seen from the net deviations in
Table 22, that pre-1975 immigrants have
significantly higher fertility than that of non-
Spanish origin whites in all age groups. This
is particularly interesting considering the lack
of a pattern in the mean values for this group
in Table 20. The effects of disruption are
again evident for post-1975 immigrants. Their
cumulative fertility is actually lower than that
of non-Spanish origin whites until age 25, and
from ages 25 to 29, their fertility is not
significantly different. It appears that there
has been disruption for several years prior to
their actual immigration. This result is not

126

TABLE 22.   Gross and Net Deviations in Average Number of Children Ever
            Born for Post-1975 and Pre-1975 Immigrants, Self-Reported
            Naturalized Citizens and Native-born Mexican Origin Women
            from Non-Spanish Origin White Women, Six Cohorts of
            Ever-Married Women: 1980

	AGE GROUPS					
	15-19	20-24	25-29	30-34	35-39	40-44
A. GROSS DEVIATIONS						
Post-1975	.224*	.497*	.897*	1.182*	1.630*	2.444*
Pre-1975	.417*	.761*	.881*	1.241*	1.416*	1.617*
Citizens	.278*	.442*	.914*	1.072*	1.027*	.775*
Native born	.228*	.462*	.633*	.786*	1.068*	1.167*
Constant	.534	.844	1.283	1.874	2.384	2.870
R^2	.022	.061	.080	.101	.105	.100
B. NET DEVIATIONS						
Post-1975	-.124	-.185*	.074	.229*	.532*	1.390*
Pre-1975	.271*	.296*	.273*	.341*	.512*	.602*
Citizens	.125	.056	.561*	.210*	.479*	.071
Native born	.235	.374*	.501*	.421*	.739*	.760*
Constant	-.269	-.929	-.656	.377	-.775	-.262
R^2	.099	.223	.245	.238	.211	.177

*significant at p=.01

127

TABLE 23. Gross and **Net** Deviations in Average Number of Children Under Three for Post-1975 and Pre-1975 Immigrants, Self-reported Naturalized Citizens and Native-born Mexican Origin Women from Non-Spanish Origin White Women, Six Cohorts of Ever-Married Women: 1980

	15-19	20-24	25-29	30-34	35-39	40-44
			AGE GROUPS			
			A. GROSS DEVIATIONS			
Post-1975	.135*	.279*	.176*	.186*	.187*	.081*
Pre-1975	.368*	.328*	.120*	.174*	.173*	.086*
Citizens	.170	.205*	.106*	.122*	.106*	.054*
Native-born	.212*	.190*	.047*	.039*	.059*	.022*
Constant	.412	.452	.419	.256	.086	.020
R^2	.020	.029	.007	.014	.027	.018
			B. NET DEVIATIONS			
Post-1975	-.070	.035	.065	.105*	.116*	.086*
Pre-1975	.274*	.186*	.045	.115*	.118*	.087*
Citizens	.056	.073	.083*	.064	.059*	.066*
Native-born	.209	.163*	.037	-.004	.026	.027*
Constant	.277	.849	1.134	1.451	1.179	.265
R^2	.052	.086	.052	.050	.053	.029

*significant at p=.01

128

surprising as the husband is likely to have preceded the wife in going to the U.S. and may have been in the U.S. since before 1975. The higher cumulative fertility in the older reproductive ages again reflects the longer exposure to the fertility norms of Mexico. Naturalized citizens have significantly higher fertility in only three age groups (25-29, 30-34, and 35-39).

The current fertility pattern shown in Table 23 largely reflects that pattern observed in Table 22. Pre-1975 immigrants have significantly higher fertility than that of non-Spanish origin whites in all but one age group (25-29). Fertility is significantly higher for post-1975 immigrants only after age 30, and is even lower than that of non-Spanish origin whites from ages 15 to 19. Naturalized citizens have significantly higher fertility in age groups 25-29, 35-39, and 40-44.

DISCUSSION

These results support the hypothesis that disruption is particularly evident among recent immigrants, who are also most likely to be illegal aliens. Naturalized citizens are most likely to have assimilated and their fertility deviates only slightly from that of other whites. The pre-1975 immigrants are most likely to be legal aliens, but represent a heterogeneous group, particularly in comparison to the post-1975 immigrants and naturalized citizens. This fertility deviation from non-Spanish origin whites indicate little, if any of the effects of either disruption or assimilation.

Because the pre-1975 immigrants have come to the United States over a 40-year time span, it would seem likely that the year of immigration would affect fertility. The results of the regression equations for children ever born and children under three are shown in Table 24, with period of immigration included as a

Table 24. Net Deviations[1] in **Average Number** of Children Ever Born and Children Under Three for Post-1975 and Pre-1975 Immigrants, Self-reported Naturalized Citizens and Native-born Mexican Origin Women from Non-Spanish Origin White Women, Six Cohorts of Ever-married Women: 1980

	AGE GROUPS					
	15-19	20-24	25-29	30-34	35-39	40-44
A. CHILDREN EVER BORN						
Post-1975	-.115	-.229*	.082	.243*	.536*	1.479*
Pre-1975	.294	.191*	.294*	.381*	.526*	1.026*
Citizens	.149	-.053	.585*	.259*	.497*	.619*
Native-born	.235*	.373*	.501*	.421*	.738*	.739*
Constant	-.270	-.927	-.657	.364	-.778	-.214
R²	.099	.223	.245	.238	.211	.181
B. CHILDREN UNDER THREE						
Post-1975	-.038	.017	.046	.122*	.121*	.091*
Pre-1975	.356*	.143*	-.006	.162*	.137*	.111*
Citizen	.144	.028	.024	.123*	.083*	.097*
Native-born	.211*	.162*	.376	-.004	.025	.026*
Constant	.273	.850	1.135	1.437	1.175	.268
R²	.053	.086	.053	.051	.053	.030

*significant at p=.01

[1]Net deviations include: age, education, marital status, urban/rural residence, family income, employment experience, and period of immigration.

control variable. The magnitude of the
coefficients changed very little. Thus,
disruption and assimilation appear to have an
effect on fertility that is not affected much by
period of immigration. If the exact year of
immigration were available, there might be more
of an effect, but at this point we can only
conclude that period of immigration has a much
smaller effect on fertility than had been
expected. From this analysis, it can be seen
that the legality of the woman at the time of
and subsequent to the immigration is more
important in mediating the effects of disruption
and selectivity on fertility than when the woman
immigrated.

HYPOTHESIZED RELATIONSHIPS OF COUNTRY OF
EDUCATION ON FERTILITY

In the previous chapters of this study,
education has been included as a control
variable in the statistical models employed to
analyze the data. From hierarchical regression
results, it is evident that education exerts, in
fact, substantial influence on fertility. In
this portion of the analysis education is
examined in more detail to determine the effect
of country of education on fertility. Because
the U.S. census data do not indicate country of
education, a variable was constructed using age
at interview, year of entry to the U.S., and
level of education. Unfortunately year of entry
is not precisely known: only five-year time
spans are given. Where country of schooling can
not be determined, cohorts are coded as having
indeterminate country of education. Further
details on the construction of these variables
are included in Appendix B. Also it was not
possible to distinguish with certainty women who
were educated in the United States in the two
oldest age groups because of the broad time
spans given for time of immigration.
Using these country of education
categories, it is expected that fertility will

131

be lowest for Mexican origin women educated in the U.S. and highest for women educated in Mexico, with the indeterminate category showing intermediate levels. This hypothesis is based on school being an extremely effective means of transmitting norms and assimilating new immigrants into the host culture.

RESULTS

The means for education and the two fertility variables are shown in Table 25 by age group for the three educational groups. (See Table 10 for mean values for the native-born women.) The mean levels of education do not follow the expected pattern of the highest education recorded among U.S.-education women, followed by the indeterminate-education category, and Mexican-educated women. Instead, the indeterminate education group has the highest educational levels, probably because these women were largely educated in the United States. Support for the ad hoc hypothesis can be seen in the rather dramatic drop in mean levels of education for the indeterminate-education group from ages 30-34 to 35-39 (11.42 to 8.73 years), when U.S.-educated women no longer can be distinguished. Another explanation for the high levels of education among the indeterminate-education groups is that selectivity is a factor and these women come to the United States to complete their education.

The children ever born measure also follows this pattern, with the indeterminate-education women having the fewest children ever born. What is particularly interesting is that the cumulative fertility of Mexican-educated women is almost the same as U.S.-educated women from ages 15 to 29, even though education levels are approximately four years lower for the Mexican-educated women.

The children under three measure reflects the effect of disruption on the Mexican-educated group, most specifically in the youngest ages.

132

Table 25. Means for Selected Variables by Likely Country of Education for First-Generation Mexican Origin Women in the United States, Six Cohorts of Ever-Married Women: 1980

Variable	Age Groups					
	15-19	20-24	25-29	30-34	35-39	40-44
Mexican Educated						
Education	6.16	6.72	6.89	7.31	6.80	6.80
CEB	.82	1.44	2.24	3.18	3.86	4.40
Child <3	.58	.73	.57	.45	.27	.10
N	267	1463	2073	2042	1469	1519
Indeterminate Country of Education						
Education	10.58	11.31	11.82	11.42	8.73	9.81
CEB	.72	1.39	1.87	2.54	3.19	3.75
Child <3	.64	.80	.47	.28	.13	.08
N	102	310	316	280	371	143
U.S. Educated						
Education	9.54	10.95	11.47	10.03	--	--
CEB	.91	1.43	2.09	2.62	--	--
Child <3	.68	.67	.51	.28	--	--
N	106	199	188	78	--	--

133

The differences in the current fertility measure among the three groups are quite small (except for Mexican-educated women aged 30-34 and 35-39), which indicates that the pace of current fertility is fairly similar for these women.

The regression results are shown in Table 26 for children ever born and Table 27 for children under three. Again, the net deviations control for age, education, marital status, region, urban/rural residence, family income, and employment experience. The net deviations in Table 26 indicate some interesting patterns. Mexican-educated women have a significant negative fertility deviation in ages 20-24, but significantly positive in all older age groups, which again indicates some disruption in the younger age groups. The indeterminate-education group deviates positively and significantly from ages 20-39, and has the largest deviation of any of the three educational groups in the 20-24 and 30-34 age groups. The U.S.-educated women deviate significantly from ages 15 to 29.

In Table 27 less than half of the age/education cohorts have significantly different current fertility from that of non-Spanish origin white women. For U.S.-educated women, only ages 20-24 have significantly higher fertility than non-Spanish origin whites, only ages 15-19, 20-24, and 40-44 for indeterminate education, and ages 25-44 for Mexican-educated women. This seems to indicate that once country of education is controlled, the pace of current fertility in the first generation differs very little from that of non-Spanish origin whites. An interesting finding of Table 27 is evident in its comparison to Table 19 (Chapter 7) where the first generation is examined in the aggregate. In Table 19, the children under three measure for the first generation deviates significantly in all ages except 15-19. It appears that when the first generation is taken as a whole, this important effect of education is masked.

The most significant finding of Table 26 and 27 is that disruption has an effect on

134

TABLE 26.　Gross and Net Deviations in Average Number of Children Ever
　　　　　 Born for First-Generation Mexican Origin Women by Probable
　　　　　 Country of Education and Native-born Mexican Origin Women
　　　　　 from Non-Spanish Origin Whites, Six Cohorts of
　　　　　 Ever-Married Women: 1980

	AGE GROUPS					
	15-19	20-24	25-29	30-34	35-39	40-44
A. GROSS DEVIATIONS						
Country of Education						
Mexico	.286*	.592*	.952*	1.312*	1.472*	1.522*
Indet.	.181*	.546*	.590*	.671*	.804*	.872*
U.S.	.3ᴜ1*	.582*	.807*	.749*	--	--
Native born	.228*	.459*	.632*	.787*	1.064*	1.161*
Constant	.533	.848	1.284	1.873	2.388	2.876
R^2	.022	.057	.082	.107	.106	.090
B. NET DEVIATIONS						
Country of Education						
Mexico	-.169	-.174*	.182*	.334*	.520*	.512*
Indet.	.196	.483*	.600*	.367*	.466*	.407
U.S.	.233*	.412*	.694*	.002	--	--
Native Born	.234*	.362*	.496*	.434*	737*	.730*
Constant	-.324	.945	-.664	.320	-.787	-.309
R^2	.010	.227	.245	.239	.211	.171

*significant at $p=.01$

135

TABLE 27. Gross and Net Deviations in Average Number of Children
           Under Three for First-Generation Mexican Origin Women
           by Probable Country of Education and Native-Born Mexican
           Origin Women from Non-Spanish Origin Whites, Six Cohorts
           of Ever-Married Women: 1980

	AGE GROUPS					
	15-19	20-24	25-29	30-34	35-39	40-44
A. GROSS DEVIATIONS						
Country of Education						
Mexico	.164*	.276*	.149*	.188*	.181*	.076*
Indet.	.228*	.344*	.053*	.025	.045*	.064*
U.S.	.265*	.216*	.094*	.025	--	--
Native Born	.212*	.187*	.047*	.038*	.057*	.022*
Constant	.412	.455	.419	.258	.087	.020
R^2	.017	.028	.007	.015	.027	.017
B. NET DEVIATIONS						
Country of Education						
Mexico	-.112	.017	.059*	.125*	.121*	.079*
Indet.	.222*	.278*	.044	.003	.016	.061*
U.S.	.153	.153*	.113	-.035	--	--
Native Born	.205*	.155*	.039	-.003	.025	.025*
Constant	.209	.853	1.131	1.412	1.168	.269
R^2	.052	.087	.052	.051	.054	.028

*significant at p=.01

136

fertility over and above any education factor,
particularly in the younger ages. Current and
cumulative fertility are lower for Mexican-
educated women aged 15-24 than that for
comparable non-Spanish origin women. Although
disruption keeps cumulative fertility low, the
Mexican-educated women do not quickly assimilate
the fertility norms of the U.S. that tend to
concentrate childbearing between ages 20 and 34.
That is, their current fertility is
substantially higher than that of non-Spanish
origin women from ages 25-44. The disruption
effect is powerful in the early reproductive
ages and, because of the strength of the
disruption, the effects remain in place
throughout the childbearing years, even though
the Mexican-educated women continue their
childbearing for a longer period of time than
non-Spanish origin whites. Two factors that are
proxies for exposure to risk of pregnancy that
would be likely to confound these findings are:
age at marriage and year of immigration.

Similar to the immigrant analysis above,
year of immigration had no discernible effect on
this analysis of probable country of education.
This was surprising because year of immigration
was a key component built into the education
categories and one would expect year of
immigration to have an independent effect on
fertility. Age at marriage also would be
expected to affect fertility, but the
regressions with age at marriage included as a
control variable were very similar to the net
results presented in Tables 26 and 27.

SUMMARY

In this chapter two compositional factors
for first-generation Mexican origin women have
been examined at length: immigrant status and
probable country of education. These are
important factor in a fertility study because:
1) the first generation is a heterogeneous
population and 2) the Mexican-origin population

in 1980 contained a different mixture of immigrants than had ever before been in the United States. This analysis shows that it is beneficial to disaggregate the first-generation into various subpopulations. For instance, the cumulative fertility deviations vary greatly among the three legality categories and also among the three education groups.

The findings show strong evidence of disruption, particularly obvious in the younger ages of post-1975 immigrants and Mexican-educated women. The disruption effects are strong enough in the younger ages that there is a lifetime effect on cumulative fertility for these women.

There is also evidence of assimilation, particularly among the self-reported naturalized citizens. Immigrant status and country of education have also been shown here to have effects on fertility that are not mediated by two proxies for exposure to risk of pregnancy: age at marriage and year of immigration.

Thus, it is important to examine Mexican-origin women by age and generation categories, and also to examine the first generation by immigrant status and country of education in order to more precisely determine the effects of disruption and assimilation on cumulative and current fertility.

CHAPTER 9

SUMMARY AND CONCLUSIONS

This research has investigated the effect
of immigration on fertility levels of Mexican
origin women. To achieve this end, this study
has been organized around four basic goals.
First, the historical overview of the Mexican
American population was presented in order to
derive a theoretical framework for this study.
Three theoretical approaches were considered,
with assimilation chosen as the most appropriate
theory for the current study. Next, three
processes associated with immigration and
immigrant behavior--selectivity, disruption, and
assimilation--were discussed in relation to six
research topics, and nine hypotheses were
developed. Third, the issue of selectivity was
examined in a comparison of Mexican women and
first-generation Mexican origin women in the
United States. Fourth, the effects of
disruption were studied in a number of ways.
The Mexican origin population was disaggregated
by age, generation, immigrant status, and
country of education in order to determine the
effects of disruption and assimilation on
Mexican origin women's fertility.

The historical review in Chapter Two traced
the flow of Mexican immigration to the United
States in order to understand the current
socioeconomic position of the Mexican origin
population. As early as the 1700s the Mexican
population in the Southwest was quite diverse
socioeconomically and politically. Although the
Mexican origin population constituted a large
percentage of the total population in the
Southwest during the eighteenth and nineteenth
centuries, it was not until after 1900 that
large numbers of Mexican immigrants came to the
United States.

There have been three very distinct periods
of Mexican immigration to the U.S. during the
20th century: 1900-1929, 1930-1964, and 1965-

1989. The first period was marked by large
numbers of immigrants coming to work in the
newly irrigated farmlands. The second period,
1930-1964, was originally a time of reduced
immigration owing to the depression, but World
War II created a labor demand that was met in
part by the Bracero program. Discontinuation of
the Bracero program in 1964 marked the beginning
of the third immigration period. The United
States' immigration policy has attempted to
impose stricter controls on immigration during
the last 30 years through legislation such as
the Immigration Reform and Control Act of 1986.
From this historical review we conclude that: 1)
immigration of the Mexican origin population has
been primarily voluntary in nature; 2) the
majority of the immigrants have come to the
United States during the twentieth century; and
3) the Mexican origin population has always
been, and continues to be, quite diverse.

    Three theoretical frameworks that are
commonly used in studies of immigrant groups
were presented in Chapter Three: colonialism,
cultural pluralism, and assimilation. A number
of other theoretical perspectives have been used
in previous studies of the Mexican origin
population. Several of these theories fall into
the rubric of labor-based theories such as the
dual economy and the split labor market
hypothesis. Because this research has explored
sociological and demographic issues related to
the Mexican origin population, rather than
economic issues, the economic theories were not
considered as possible frameworks for this
study.

    The first theory that was examined for this
study was colonialism theory. However, its
emphasis on the involuntary nature of the
presence of Mexican origin persons in the United
States diluted its usefulness. As seen in
Chapter Two, this scenario might have described
a small fraction of the Mexican origin
population at some point in time, but it is not

140

particularly appropriate to the current-day situation.

The second theoretical approach considered was cultural pluralism, which emphasizes eventual equality of racial/ethnic groups, but does not explain behavioral changes of immigrants. Assimilation theory does not assume either involuntary immigration or equality. However, assimilation theory allows for behavioral change to occur over time, as exposure to values and norms of the host country increases.

Assimilation was chosen as the theoretical framework for this study because it is concerned with how immigration affects fertility-- specifically how fertility behavior of women changes over time--and is less concerned with the political aspects of subordination and equality.

Assimilation theory predicts that the longer immigrants are in the host country, the more likely they are to assume the norms and values of that country. However, support for assimilation theory as applied to fertility research has been inconsistent in the case of the Mexican origin population. Some studies have found evidence that the Mexican origin population has assimilated the lower fertility norms of the U.S., while other studies have not. These discrepancies are due in part to some studies utilizing current fertility as the dependent variable, while others have looked at cumulative fertility. Another possible reason for the disparate results has been an emphasis on the behavioral changes of immigrants once in the host country, but some of the processes that occur temporally prior to the move have not been examined.

The assimilation framework is supplemented in this study to include two processes that could impact on fertility of immigrant women: selectivity and disruption. In Chapter Four the effects of selectivity, disruption, and assimilation on fertility of Mexican origin women were developed in terms of six research topics and in nine research hypotheses. The following chapters examine these research hypotheses.

SUPPORT FOR THE SELECTIVITY HYPOTHESIS

Chapter Five is the only chapter that deals directly with selectivity. Because selectivity refers to women in the country of origin, Mexican women are used as the comparison group for this portion of the analysis. Basic demographic information and a discussion of Mexico's population policy during the 1970s were presented to determine if selectivity could have been confounded by the dramatic fertility decline during the 1970s in Mexico. The hypotheses that were examined in this chapter were as follows:

1.   Immigration is selective of Mexicans who have higher socioeconomic status and education levels.

2.   Mexican immigration women will have fertility levels lower than that of women remaining in Mexico.

3.   In addition to selectivity, fertility levels of women migrating to the United States between 1975 and 1980 should further reflect the lower fertility norms of Mexico, and have lower fertility than other Mexican immigrants who arrived prior to 1975.

The first hypothesis was supported in a comparison of Mexican and first-generation Mexican origin women in the United States.

142

The immigrant women had on average over two years more education than urban Mexican women and over four years more than rural Mexican women. There were not any other directly comparable socioeconomic variables available, but the education variable strongly supports selectivity.

In support of the second hypothesis, both current and cumulative fertility were much lower for the first-generation women than the Mexican women. The mean number of children ever born for rural Mexican women aged 40-44 was 7.91, for urban Mexican women 6.44, and Mexican immigrant women in the U.S. 4.34. As cumulative fertility for this age group approximates completed childbearing, it can be seen that rural Mexican women have almost twice as many children as Mexican immigrant women in the U.S. Urban Mexican women have about two more children than Mexican immigrants to the U.S.

Support for the third hypothesis was not apparent in the data. Only at ages 15-19 and 20-24 was fertility lower of recent immigrant women lower. Thus, the lower fertility norms of Mexico were not yet evident in the fertility levels of recent immigrant women. This may be a result in part of the composition of the recent immigrant population. A large portion of the illegals counted in the 1980 Census came to the U.S. in the 1970s, so immigrant status may be a confounding factor. Also, there may not have been enough time elapsed between the new population policies in Mexico and the Census date for the lower fertility norms to be apparent. This may be more discernible in the 1990 Census than it was in 1980. It may be concluded, therefore, that immigration to the U.S. from Mexico is positively selective and that the immigrant women have much lower fertility than women remaining in Mexico.

DISRUPTION

Chapters Seven and Eight utilized U.S. census data to explore the effects of disruption and assimilation on fertility of Mexican origin women. In Chapter Seven, the women were disaggregated by age and generational status in a comparison of 1970 and 1980 Census data. In Chapter Eight, the first-generation women were divided into groups by immigrant status and probable country of education. The women were separated into these various groups so that the effects of disruption and assimilation could be better understood, given that a number of other variables may confound those effects. The first three research hypotheses guiding this portion of the research were:

1. Owing to the physical and/or social disruption of the move, disruption will have the effect of lowering fertility around the time of the immigration.

2. The longer the disruption, the lower the fertility of the immigrants.

3. Mexican origin women partially make-up for their postponed or delayed fertility owing to the short-term effects of the disruption, but their cumulative fertility levels will continue to reflect the disruptive effect to some degree.

The disruption effects were quite strong in each of the subpopulation analyses. In 1970 and 1980, cumulative and current fertility levels were generally lower for first-generation women than for native-born women and in some ages lower than that of non-Spanish origin whites, once the control variables were included in the regression analysis. The disruption effect was again very strong in the analysis of immigrant

144

status. The post-1975 immigrants had lower
fertility than non-Spanish origin white women
from ages 15-24 for cumulative fertility, and
ages 15-19 for current fertility. This same
pattern was true of Mexican-educated women.
These two groups of women--post-1975 immigrants
and Mexican-educated--are likely to contain a
large proportion of illegal immigrants, so it
appears that disruption has a large effect on
illegals. This is consistent with the notion
that there is a great deal of circular migration
among this group and that it may be quite common
for the husband to precede the remainder of the
family in going to the U.S.[1] Unfortunately, a
specific measure was not available as to the
time spouses were separated or of social
disruption, so it was impossible to directly
address the second hypothesis that the longer
the disruption, the greater the effect.
However, these data strongly support the first
and third hypotheses. Disruption does have an
obvious immediate short-term effect in lowering
current fertility, but there is also a long-term
effect resulting in lower cumulative fertility
because the immigrant women never fully regain
their delayed childbearing.

SUPPORT FOR THE ASSIMILATION HYPOTHESIS

The second set of hypotheses examined in
Chapters Seven and Eight were those related to
assimilation. The three hypotheses were:

1.   Fertility is lower with increasing
      time in the host country. Thus,
      native-born Mexican origin women are
      expected to have lower fertility than
      first-generation Mexican women.

2.   Assimilation is expected to be a major
      factor in lowering fertility among
      legal immigrants and naturalized
      citizens, but disruption is expected

to have a larger effect among illegal
migrants.

3.   Assimilation is expected to be most
      effective in lowering fertility among
      Mexican origin women who are educated
      in the United States.

Evidence for the first hypothesis had been found
in previous studies (Bean et al., 1984), and was
again supported in this study. As was evident
in Figures 7-10, the mean values for children
ever born and children under three were lower
for native-born than for first-generation
Mexican origin women. The gross deviations in
Tables 16-19 were the actual fertility
deviations of each generation from non-Spanish
origin whites and showed the expected pattern of
assimilation, in that fertility was lower for
the native-born women than for the first-
generation women.

However, once the control variables were
included in the regression equations, another
pattern emerged. That is, once education was
controlled statistically, the fertility patterns
were changed. The effect of assimilation on
fertility was evident in the children under
three measure in 1980 (Table 19); in both 1970
and 1980, the cumulative fertility deviations
for native-born women from that of non-Spanish
origin whites were higher in all but one age
group of the first-generation Mexican origin
women. This result may once again indicate the
strength of disruption. In other words, in a
comparison of native-born and first-generation
Mexican origin women, the effects of disruption
may be so strong in the first generation that
the effects of assimilation may be overshadowed
when levels of education are controlled.

Support for this ad hoc hypothesis can be
found in the cohort comparison in Chapter Seven
(Table 20). Effects of disruption were apparent
in both the children under three and children
ever born measures of the first-generation women

146

in 1970, but by 1980, first-generation women had
higher current fertility than native-born
Mexican origin women. Cumulative fertility
deviations were still lower for the first-
generation than native-born Mexican origin women
but the deviations for the first-generation
women were all positive and significant in 1980.
The short-term effects of disruption were
evident in both fertility measures in 1970, as
well as the long-term effects on cumulative
fertility in 1980. However, there was also
evidence of assimilation among the native-born
women, particularly in the current fertility
measure in 1980. Among the native-born women
there was only one age group in 1980 (40-44
years of age) that showed current fertility that
deviated significantly from that of non-Spanish
origin whites. This indicates that the pace of
fertility of native-born women is very similar
to that of non-Spanish origin whites and that
the native-born women have accepted the
fertility norms of the U.S.

The second hypothesis was examined in
Chapter Eight. Legal immigrants, illegal
immigrants, and naturalized citizens could not
be distinguished directly using the census data,
so proxies were utilized to divide the first-
generation Mexican origin women: post-1975 and
pre-1975 immigrants, and self-reported
naturalized citizens. Although these groups are
not exact matches with legal status of
immigrants, they are useful in determining
patterns.

The mean values for children ever born and
children under three were generally lower for
the naturalized-citizens than for post-1975 or
pre-1975 immigrants, but the differences in the
values for children under three were minimal
among the three groups. The differences in
cumulative fertility for the three groups did
diverge with age. Naturalized citizens aged
40-44 had over one and a half children less than
post-1975 immigrants, and over a child less than
pre-1975 immigrants. Once the control variables

147

were included in the regression equations, self-reported naturalized citizens generally had smaller fertility deviations than the pre-1975 immigrants for both current and cumulative fertility. Once again the disruptive effects were quite evident, particularly among the post-1975 immigrants. This again had the effect of overshadowing the effects of assimilation in the within-group comparison, although there is some evidence of assimilation among the self-reported naturalized citizens.

The third hypothesis was examined also in Chapter Eight. The first-generation Mexican origin women were disaggregated into groups by country of education: U.S., Mexico, or indeterminate. The mean values showed little difference among the three groups for the children under three measure; the indeterminate education group had the lowest mean values of children ever born. The net deviations from the regression equations again showed domination by the disruption effect, particularly in the younger reproductive ages. Perhaps owing to the inability to determine precisely where women received their education, there was not much evidence of assimilation among the U.S.-educated women. It is possible that many of the women in the indeterminate-education group actually received the majority of their education in the United States and may be showing signs of assimilation, but this cannot be determined without knowing more about this group.

In conclusion, there is evidence of assimilation in the Mexican origin population. The native-born women in 1980 have current fertility levels similar to that of non-Spanish origin white women. There is also some evidence of assimilation among self-reported naturalized citizens, U.S.-educated women, and mixed country of education women. In all of these intergroup comparisons, disruption effects have also been evident and it has not been possible to distinguish the two effects on fertility in some instances. However, all three hypotheses

148

were supported by the findings presented in Chapters Seven and Eight.

CONCLUSION AND FUTURE STUDIES

This study has examined the complex interrelationships of selectivity, disruption, and assimilation, and how they alter the fertility behavior of immigrant and native-born Mexican origin women. To this end, we have looked at several dimensions of these relationships.[2] Changes over time and across generations were examined in Chapter Seven, and changes within the foreign born generation in Chapters Six and Eight. Individual level characteristics were examined in Chapters Six and Seven; structural characteristics such as country of education were examined in Chapter Eight.

Evidence of selectivity, disruption, and assimilation affecting fertility behavior have been detected. It is not possible to determine the absolute strength of one over the others in lowering fertility, but the relative strengths of the three may be summarized. There is no question that selectivity is operative and that the women immigrating to the United States from Mexico are positively selected. Also, there is strong evidence of assimilation when looking at the mean or gross levels of fertility. However, when the control variables are included in the regression equation, most specifically education, it is disruption that is most evident. This is particularly true in the case of the children ever born measure. Thus it appears that disruption has the strongest effect on fertility within the first generation, but that selectivity and assimilation also have effects that cannot be ignored.

Although nearly all of the research hypotheses were supported by the findings of this analysis, some questions remain unanswered. Future research could contribute to the study of immigration and fertility by developing better measures of some of the variables. For instance, it is evident that disruption has a major effect on fertility of Mexican origin women. Spousal separation may account for a large portion of this disruption effect, and yet the length or frequency of spousal separation could not be determined. It would be much more difficult to measure social disruption, but again, this would be extremely useful in a study such as this. The immigrant status and country of education analyses might show more evident patterns if we could more precisely measure or determine immigrant status and country of origin. The analyses presented here have been very useful in gaining some knowledge as to how the first generation is differentially affected, pointing to the need for more precise measures.

This analysis has attempted to separate the effects of selectivity, disruption, and assimilation on fertility. This has been illuminating, but difficult in that the three processes are so closely intertwined. It would be useful to examine the interrelationships of the three processes in future studies in order to determine how the effects are muted or magnified by one another. It will also be interesting to see in what manner selectivity, disruption, and assimilation are evident in lowering fertility of the Mexican origin population in 1990. The 1990 Census will provide an excellent opportunity to continue the cohort analysis, as the volume of immigration from Mexico to the U.S. was high again in the 1980s. Some of the results from 1980 were clouded by the presence of the large numbers of illegals in the census. Perhaps the 1990 Census will be able to distinguish that group to better determine the effects of immigration on their fertility. Although these and other questions await future analysis, the results presented in this study suggest the utility of examining the crossroads Mexican origin women face as they move from one country to another, from one culture to another.

FOOTNOTES

CHAPTER 2

1.   The lands were obtained through rebellion in
part of Texas (the Battle of San Jacinto in
1830), warfare in New Mexico and Texas, and
purchase of parts of Arizona and New Mexico (the
Gadsden Purchase of 1853).

2.   The number of immigrants in Texas exceeded
7,000 by 1830, compared to 3,000 Mexicans
(Weber, 1982).

3.   Bancroft (as cited in McWilliams, 1968)
estimated that 2,000 Mexicans were living in San
Antonio, 1,400 at La Bahia, and 500 in
Nacogdoches, with the remaining 1,100 spread out
in smaller missions or border towns.

4.   The number of immigrants did drop in 1917
owing to the literacy test and head tax required
by the Immigration Act of February 5, 1917.   The
growers immediately pressed for this to be
rescinded and on May 23, 1917, Secretary of
Labor Wilson issued a departmental order that
waived the literacy test and head tax for
Mexican agricultural workers (Reisler, 1976).
The order was eventually amended to stipulate
workers could only stay six months.   The
temporary admissions program was in effect until
March 1921.

5.   Included in the 1924 Immigration Act was the
establishment of the border patrol.   Congress
appropriated $1 million to fund a 450-person
patrol to guard the Canadian and Mexican
borders.

6.   Only 2 percent of the nation's commercial
farmers had bracero workers (Hawley, 1966).

7. In 1980, 34.5 percent of the Mexican origin population was under age 15, compared to 22.6 percent of the total U.S. population (Bean, Stephen, and Opitz, 1985). The total fertility rate per 1000 Mexican origin women was 2886.5 versus 1689.5 for non-Hispanic white women aged 15-44 in 1980 (Ventura, 1983).

CHAPTER 3

1. The population in the Southwest was very young: 45 percent of Santa Fe's population was under age 16 in 1845. Other cities in New Mexico had even younger populations such as Abiquiu (48 percent under 16) and Lode Mora (50 percent). Texas had a slightly older population in 1833 with 42.2 percent of the population under 16 in Nacogdoches, Goliad, and San Antonio. In the northeastern portion of the United States, 42 percent of the population was under age 15 in 1830 (Weber, 1982: 217). The young population in the Southwest indicates that high fertility rates had existed for some time and, as these children moved into childbearing years, there would be continued high rates of fertility. High levels of fertility occurred in California where it has been estimated that women had an average of 10 children (Pitt, 1967). Bradshaw and Bean (1972) found that in 1850 married, spouse-present women of Spanish surname age 15 to 49 living in San Antonio had about one-third more children under age five (2,040 per 1000 women) than did similar other white women (1,543).

2. Park and Burgess have defined some of these terms as follows:

> Accommodation -- a process of adjustment, that is, an organization of social relations and attitudes to present or to reduce conflict, to control competition, and to maintain a basis of security in the social order for persons and groups of

divergent interests and types to carry on
together their varied lifestyles.

Assimilation -- a process of
interpenetration and fusion in which
persons and groups acquire the memories,
sentiments, and attitudes of other persons
or groups, and by sharing their experience
and history, are incorporated with them in
a common cultural life (Park and Burgess,
1969: 360).

CHAPTER 4

1. For instance, social and economic factors
were important in the increase in the birth rate
during the baby boom of the 1950s and the
fertility decline of the 1960s and 1970s.

2. There is still disagreement in the
literature as to whether or not age, period, and
cohort effects can be separated empirically.
(See Feinberg and Mason, 1978; Glenn, 1976; and
Pullum, 1980.) The intent here, however, is not
to statistically or empirically separate the
three, but rather to identify age, period, and
cohort effects on fertility by examining age
groups and cohorts at two points in time.

3. Control variable included age, education,
labor force participation, region, family
income, marital status, and urban/rural
residence.

CHAPTER 5

1. An evaluation of the 1980 Census was
undertaken by the Census Bureau to determine if
there was misreporting in the Mexican American
category in certain areas of the country (U.S.
Bureau of the Census, 1982). Misreporting was
suspected because of some unexpected
distributions of the Mexican origin population
and matches with administrative record indicated

possible misreporting. It appeared to be most common in the South and the Northeast, but not in the Southwest. The study concluded that the misreporting was most severe in parts of the country where the Spanish origin is sparse and that almost one-third of the total Mexican population in the study areas was misreported, resulting in 109,000 white Mexican and 103,000 black Mexican responses being rejected. Again, it must be emphasized that this misreporting was not detected in the southwestern states and should not adversely affect this study. Furthermore, it is estimated that over one million undocumented immigrants were included in the 1980 Census, who were not counted in the 1970 Census (Warren and Passel, 1987). For the 1970 to 1980 comparisons, it is important to keep in mind the existence of the illegals in the 1980 counts.

2. Ever-married includes women who are currently married, widowed, divorced, or separated. A marriage in the United States is defined as the legal sanction of a marriage; in Mexico consensual unions are fairly common and are generally considered the equivalent of marriage (World Fertility Survey, 1980). Because the respondents self-report this item on the census, it is not known for certainty, but it is expected that Mexican-origin respondents living in a consensual union would report themselves as married in the United States census.

3. Bean and Swicegood (1985) computed ratios of own-children to the 1979 vital statistics, which resulted in slightly smaller ratios at every age. Their rationale for using the 1979 vital statistics stemmed from: 1) comparability of ratios computed using 1970 Census and 1969 vital statistics; 2) that the 1980 vital statistics are from a sample registration area; and 3) that three-fourths of the children under age one in the census would have been born in 1979.

However, all five southwestern states are included in the sample registration area and because it is possible to specifically delineate the Mexican origin population in the 1980 data, the ratios shown in Table 2 would appear to more accurately reflect the population of interest, presuming that birth rates were relatively constant for the Mexican origin population from 1979 to 1980. Bean and Swicegood also evaluated the own-children measure of cumulative fertility from the 1980 Census by computing ratios of own children under the age of 15 to children ever born. For both other whites and Mexican Americans, the ratios ranged from .89 to .95 from ages 15 to 34. After age 35, the ratios dropped dramatically indicating that children were older than age 15 and/or had moved out of the household. Prior to age 35, there is strong evidence that the own-children under age 15 measure is a reliable measure of cumulative fertility. Bean and Swicegood reported that the cumulative fertility for Mexican Americans was less than for other whites, indicating that Mexican Americans are slightly less likely to have children living at home whether it is a cause of mortality, children living with other relatives, or for some other reason.

4. A de jure definition of residence was used.

CHAPTER 6

1. The crude death rate is affected by the age structure of the population and in this case, the very young population of Mexico is reflected in the low crude death rate. For instance the crude death rate in the United States in 1980 (8.9) was higher than that of Mexico even though mortality was lower in the United States (National Center for Health Statistics, 1985). A better measure of mortality in this instance is life expectancy at birth, which was 59.4 years for males and 63.4 years for females in

Mexico in 1970 and 62.1 for males and 66.0 for females in 1979 (United Nations, 1975, 1988).

2.   Intermediate or intervening variable are characterized as those variable that mediate the effects of social structures on fertility. Davis and Blake (1956) identified 11 such variables and grouped them as: 1) the "intercourse" variables; 2) the "conception" variables; and 3) the "gestation" variables. This study examines two of these variables in Mexico: proportion marrying (an intercourse variable) and contraceptive usage (conception variable).

3.   The aberration in the youngest age group may be a result of ineffective users, or may be exaggerated by the incidence of women in family planning post partum programs. That is, women in that age group may have had a child within the last year and then accepted the family planning program immediately after the birth.

4.   There have been a number of fertility surveys undertaken in Mexico. Pullum, Casterline, and Juarez (1985) found that the 1977 World Fertility Survey and 1982 National Contraceptive Study were of very high quality and no inconsistencies were reported.

5.   Own children under age three is utilized in the following analyses for the United States as a measure of current fertility and is a preferable measure to children under five. However, children under five was the only own children measure available for Mexico, so for comparison purposes, it is utilized in the selectivity section.

6.   In Mexico primary is six years, secondary is three years, and preparatory or vocational schooling is three years.

7.   This comparison includes only first-generation women in the United States. In Chapter Seven data are provided for second- or higher-generation women also.

CHAPTER 7

1.   In 1970, the definition of urbanized areas required a central city of 50,000 population or twin cities to have a combined population of 50,000 with the smaller city having a population of at least 15,000.   In 1980 there was no minimum population size required for the central city.   Although the urban/rural definition basically did not change between 1970 and 1980, the 1980 coding differed from 1970 when residence was simply coded as a dichotomy: urban or rural.   In 1980, urban was coded as urban city or suburban lot, place of less than one acre, vacant unity, or group quarters. Rural was coded as all rural nonfarms and rural farms.   The latter population consists of persons living in a rural area, but not on a farm defined above.   The combination of these two rural definitions should include all persons living in rural areas, but the codebook indicates that not all rural nonfarms are included in the rural nonfarm category (U.S. Bureau of the Census, 1983c).   This will have the effect of slightly inflating the percent urban in 1980.

CHAPTER 9

1.   Massey and Mullan (1984b) found that the average stay of illegals in the U.S. was longer than legals (12.4 versus 9.4 months).

2.   This analysis has focused on the fertility of female immigrants and has not addressed the issue of couples' decision-making processes regarding fertility.   Beckman (1978) has shown that studies of joint decision-making are important, particularly when couples do not

agree regarding fertility desires. Sri Lankan data indicate that married couples who have similar family size preferences are the most likely to use contraceptives effectively (Kane, Sivasubramaniam, and Stanback, 1988). This may be an important consideration in studies of the Mexican origin population if the fertility decisions are dominated by the husband, as has been suggested by some of the literature stressing the role of machismo in the Mexican origin population. However, Hollerbach (1980) found little evidence that "men high on machismo prefer children." Men in cultures characterized by machismo may be more likely to disapprove of birth control (Beckman, 1983) and thereby influence the outcomes of fertility decisions. These data do not present an opportunity to examine questions regarding fertility decision-making, but future research could examine this issue and make an important contribution.

APPENDIX A

The sample for the 1980 panel was created at the Population Research Center at the University of Texas at Austin. The first stage of the sampling was based on the race/ethnicity of the household head on the PUMS-A. The following sampling fractions were used for households:

1/10 : non-Spanish origin white
              (Anglo)

1/2 : black

1/1 : all other

This resulted in the following number of households as categorized by the race/ethnicity of the household head:

332,745	Anglo
208,438	Black
102,636	Mexican American
29,768	Puerto Rican
14,193	Cuban
2,526	Black Hispanic
52,680	Oriental and other
21,342	American Indian
6,460	Possible Illegal
45,596	Residual

Sampling fractions were then applied to the household to create a worktape. The sampling fractions and resulting number of households are as follows:

Sampling Fraction	Households
1/10	33,274 Anglo
1/8	26,054 Black
1/4	25,659 Mexican American
1/2	14,884 Puerto Rican
1/1	14,193 Cuban
1/1	2,526 Black Hispanic
1/4	13,170 Oriental and other
1/2	10,671 American Indian
1/1	6,460 Possible Illegal
1/6	8,266 Residual

For this study, the cases were then weighted by the inverse of their sampling fraction(s) to reflect the original distribution of households on the PUMS-A. Anglos were weighted by 100 (1/10 * 1/10), and Blacks by 16 (1/2 * 1/8) to reflect the inverse of the sampling fractions that had been applied in both stages for those two groups. For all other groups, the weight was simply the inverse of the sampling fraction. For instance, American Indians were weighted by 2, since their sampling fraction had been 1/2.

This study, however, required a sample of women, not a sample of households. Sampling on the basis of the household with a household head would under or over sample women living in a household with a household head of a different race/ethnicity. A sample of approximately 30,000 Mexican origin women and 30,000 Anglo women was desired for this study, so a sampling fraction of 1/2 was used for the Mexican origin households and 1/50 for Anglo households. This resulted in a final sample of 31,291 Mexican origin women and 27,189 non-Spanish origin women. If a household head was of a different race/ethnicity than the woman, another set of weights was applied to reflect the household composition.

APPENDIX B

The variables indicating probable country of education were constructed using information on age of the woman at the time of the census, year of entry to the United States, and level of education. Women were coded as one of three groups--U.S.-educated, Mexican-educated, or indeterminate country of education--based on a cross-classification of age and period of immigration, as shown in Figure 14. For instance, women who were 15-19 in 1980 and entered the United States between 1960 and 1965 had to have received their education entirely in the United States because they would have been four at the oldest when they migrated. Because the exact year of immigration is not available, we are not able to determine for certain in what country education was received for two groups in each age cohort (except the 40-44 year olds, who had only one cohort undetermined). For the women in the mixed country of education category, amount of education was also utilized as a criterion variable. The algorithms for this computation were:

x_i = 5 + completed years of schooling
(to get age at completion of schooling)
y_i = age in 1980 - x_i
(to get years since completed schooling)

Critical values of y_i were computed based on period of immigration. Because the exact year of immigration was not known, a mid-period critical value was taken. Completed education is in whole numbers so rather than taking 2.5 as the mid-period value, 2.0 was taken as a conservative estimate. These critical values are shown in Table 28. For instance, a woman who immigrated between 1965 and 1970 and had a y_i value of 12 or more was coded as being educated in Mexico; women with y_i values less than 12 were coded as mixed education. As another example, for a 15-19 year old woman who

162

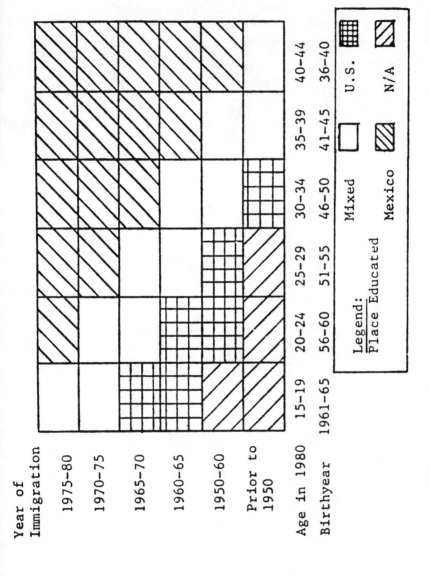

Figure 14. Diagram of Place of Education by Age and Year of Immigration

163

Table 28. Critical Values of Year of Education Used in Coding
          Probable Place of Education

Period of immigration	Critical value
1975-1980	2.0
1970-1975	7.0
1965-1970	12.0
1960-1965	17.0
1950-1960	All indeterminate
Prior to 1950	All indeterminate

immigrated between 1975 and 1980, the critical value was two, or that she had completed her schooling at least two years prior to 1980. Thus, a 15-year old woman who had eight years of education would have been coded as Mexican educated, but a 15-year old woman with nine or ten years of education was coded an indeterminate education. This coding scheme has a slight bias toward coding more women as indeterminate education. Again, if the specific year of immigration were known, many fewer women would have been in the indeterminate-education category. However, this coding was as refined as possible given the data limitations.

REFERENCES

Alarcon, Francisco. 1982. "Demographic Background." In Jorge Manatou Martinez (ed.), The Demographic Revolution in Mexico 1980-1980. Mexico City: Mexican Institute of Social Security.

Alba, Francisco. 1978. "Mexico's International Migration as a Manifestation of its Development Pattern." International Migration Review 12(4): 502-513.

_____. 1982. The Population of Mexico: Trends, Issues, and Policies. New Brunswick: Transaction Books.

Alvirez, David and Frank D. Bean. 1976. "The Mexican American Family." In C.H. Mindel and R.W. Habenstein (eds.), Ethnic Families in America: Patterns and Variations. New York: Elsevier.

Bagozzi, R.P. and M.I. van Loo. 1980. "Decision-Making and Fertility: A Theory of Exchange in the Family." In Thomas K. Burch (ed.), Demographic Behavior. Boulder: Westview Press.

Barrera, Mario. 1979. Race and Class in the Southwest: A Theory of Racial Inequality. Notre Dame, IN: University of Notre Dame Press.

Bean, Frank D. and Benjamin S. Bradshaw. 1977. "Mexican American Fertility." In Charles H. Teller, Leo F. Estrada, Jose Fernandez, and David Alvirez (eds.), Cuantos Somos: A Demographic Study of the Mexican American Population. Austin: University of Texas Press.

Bean, Frank D., Harley L. Browning and W. Parker
Frisbie. 1984. "What the 1980 United States
Census Tells Us about the Characteristics of
Illegal and Legal Mexican Immigrants."
International Migration Review 18(3): 672-691.

Bean, Frank D., Ruth M. Cullen, Elizabeth H.
Stephen and Gray Swicegood. 1984.
"Generational Differences in Fertility among
Mexican Americans: Implications for Assessing
the Effects of Immigration." Social Science
Quarterly 65(June): 573-582.

Bean, Frank D., Allan G. King and Jeffrey S.
Passel. 1983. "The Number of Illegal Migrants
of Mexican Origin in the United States: Sex
Ratio-Based Estimates for 1980." Demography
20(1): 99-109.

Bean, Frank D., Elizabeth H. Stephen and
Wolfgang Opitz. 1985. "A Demographic Profile
of the Mexican Origin Population in the United
States." In R. de la Garza, F. Bean, C.
Bonjean, R. Romo, and R. Alvarez (eds.), The
Mexican Origin Experience: An Interdisciplinary
Anthology. Austin: University of Texas Press.

Bean, Frank D. and Marta Tienda. 1987. The
Hispanic Population of the United States. New
York: Russell Sage Foundation.

Bean, Frank D. and Gray Swicegood. 1982.
"Generation, Female Education and Fertility
among Mexican Americans." Social Science
Quarterly 63(March): 131-144.

_____. 1985. Mexican American Fertility.
Austin: University of Texas Press.

Bean, Frank D., Gray Swicegood, and Thomas
Linsley. 1981. "Patterns of Fertility
Variation among Mexican Immigrants to the United
States." In U.S. Immigration Policy and the
National Interest, Staff Report, Appendix D.
Washington, D.C.: Select Commission on
Immigration and Refugee Policy.

Beckman, Linda J. 1978. "Couples' Decision-
Making Processes Regarding Fertility." In Karl
E. Taeuber, Larry Bumpass, and James A. Sweet
(eds.), Social Demography, New York, Academic
Press.

Beckman, Linda J. 1983. "Communication, Power,
and the Influence of Social Networks in Couples
Decisions on Fertility." In Rodolfo A. Bulatao
and Ronald D. Lee (eds.), Determinants of
Fertility in Developing Countries, New York:
Academic Press.

Bradshaw, Benjamin S. and Frank D. Bean. 1972.
"Some Aspects of the Fertility of Mexican
Americans." Commission on Population Growth and
the American Future, Research Reports, Volume 1.
In Charles F. Westoff and Robert Parke, Jr.
(eds.), Demographic and Social Aspects of
Population Growth, Washington, D.C.: U.S.
Government Printing Office.

Browning, Harley L. and Waltraut Feindt. 1969.
"Selectivity of Migrants to a Metropolis in a
Developing Country: A Mexican Case Study."
Demography 6(4): 347-358.

Browning, Harley L. and Ruth M. Cullen. 1983.
"The Complex Demographic Formation of the United
States Mexican Origin Population." Austin:
Texas Population Research Center Working Paper
No. 5.020.

Borjas, George J. 1982. "A Methodology for
Estimates the Extent of Labor Market Competition
Between Minority and Non-Minority Groups."
Paper presented at the Rockefeller Foundation
Workshop on Labor Market Consequences of
Immigration Policy, Wingspread Conference
Center, Racine, Wisconsin, August.

Business Week. 1983. "Bridling at a U.S.
Immigration Bill." February 28: 43-44.

Carlson, Elwood D. 1985. "The Impact of
International Migration upon Timing of Marriage
and Childbearing." Demography 22(1): 61-72.

Chapman, L.F. 1976. Statement before the
Subcommittee on Immigration and Naturalization
of the Committee of the Judiciary. United
States Congress, Ninety-fourth Congress, Second
Session, Washington, D.C., March 17.

Chaze, W.L. 1982. "Will U.S. Shut the Door on
Immigrants." U.S. News and World Report
92(April 12): 47-50.

Chiswick, Barry R. 1979. "The Economic
Progress of Immigrants: Some Apparently
Universal Patterns." In William Fellner (ed.),
Contemporary Economic Problems: 1979.
Washington, D.C.: American Enterprise Institute
for Public Policy Research.

Cho, Lee-Jay, W.H. Grabill, and Donald J. Bogue.
1970. Differential Current Fertility in the
United States. Chicago: Community and Family
Study Center.

Coale, Ansley. 1978. "Population Growth and
Economic Development: The Case of Mexico."
Foreign Affairs 56(January): 415-429.

Cornelius, Wayne A. 1978. "Mexican Migration to the United States: Causes, Consequences, and U.S. Responses." Center for International Studies, Migration and Development Group, Massachusetts Institute of Technology, July.

Covarrubias, Ana C. and Olivia Gonzalez. 1982. "Communication and Cognitive, Attitudinal and Behavioral Change in Family Planning." In Jorge Martinez Manatou (ed.), The Demographic Revolution in Mexico 1970-1979. Mexico City: Mexican Institute of Social Security.

Davis, Kingsley and Judith Blake. 1956. "Social Structure and Fertility: An Analytic Framework." Economic Development and Cultural Change 4(April): 211-235.

Easterlin, Richard. 1955. "Long Swings in U.S. Demographic and Economic Growth: Some Findings on the Historical Pattern." Demography 2: 390-507.

Engleman, Uriah Z. 1938. "A Study of Size of Families in the Jewish Population of Buffalo." University of Buffalo Series 16(November).

_____. 1951. "The Jewish Population of Charleston." Jewish Social Studies 13: 195-210.

Feinberg, S.E. and W.M. Mason. 1978. "Identification and Estimation of Age-period-cohort Models in the Analysis of Discrete Archival Data." In K.F. Schuessler (ed.), Sociological Methodology, San Francisco: Jossey-Bass.

Fischer, Nancy A. and John P. Marcum. 1984. "Ethnic Integration, Socioeconomic Status, and Fertility among Mexican Americans." Social Science Quarterly 65(June): 583-593.

Ford, Kathleen. 1982. "The Fertility of Immigrants to the United States." Unpublished paper.

_____. Forthcoming. "Duration of Residence in the United States and the Fertility of U.S. Immigrants." International Migration Review.

Frisbie, W. Parker. 1975. "Illegal Migration from Mexico to the United States: A Longitudinal Analysis." International Migration Review 9(1): 3-13.

Garrison, Helen. 1984. Contraceptive Effectiveness in Mexico. Unpublished Ph.D. dissertation. Stanford: Stanford University.

Glenn, Norval D. 1976. "Cohort Analysts' Futile Quest: Statistical Attempts to Separate Age, Period, and Cohort Effects." American Sociological Review 41: 900-904.

Goldscheider, Calvin. 1965. "Nativity, Generation, and Jewish Fertility." Sociological Analysis 26: 137-147.

_____. 1967. "Fertility of the Jews." Demography 4: 196-209.

Goldstein, Sidney. 1978. "Migration and Fertility in Thailand, 1960-1970." Canadian Studies in Population 5: 167-180.

Goldstein, Sidney and Alice Goldstein. 1983. "Migration and Fertility in Peninsular Malaysia: An Analysis Using Life History Data." Santa Monica: Rand Corporation Paper No. N-1860-AID.

Gomez-Quinones, Juan. 1974. "The First Steps: Chicano Labor Conflict and Organizing, 1920." In Manuel P. Servin (ed.), An Awakening Minority: The Mexican Americans, Second Edition, Beverly Hills, CA: Glencoe.

Gonzalez, Nancie L. 1967. <u>The Spanish Americans of New Mexico: A Distinctive Heritage</u>. Advance Report 9, Mexican-American Study Project. Los Angeles: University of California.

Gordon, Milton M. 1964. <u>Assimilation in American Life</u>. New York: Oxford University Press.

Gorwaney, Naintara, Marice D. Van Arsodol, Jr., David Heer, and Leo A. Schuerman. 1989. "Assimilation, Disruption of Selectivity? A Comparison of Alternative Hypotheses Regarding the Fertility of Immigrants in the United States." Presented at the Annual Meeting of the Population Association of America, Baltimore, MD, March 29–April 1.

Grebler, Leo. 1967. <u>The Schooling Gap: Signs of Progress</u>. Los Angeles: University of California, Los Angeles Mexican American Study Project No. 7.

Grebler, Leo, Joan W. Moore, and Ralph C. Guzman. 1970. <u>The Mexican-American People</u>. New York: Free Press.

Grenier, Gilles. 1984. "Shifts to English as Usual Language by Americans of Spanish Mother Tongue." <u>Social Science Quarterly</u> 65(2): 537–550.

Grossman, Jean Baldwin. 1982. "The Substitutability of Natives and Immigrants in Production." <u>Review of Economics and Statistics</u> 64: 596–603.

Grossman, Jean Baldwin. 1984. "Illegal Immigrants and Domestic Employment." <u>Industrial and Labor Relations Review</u> 37(January): 240–251.

Hawley, Ellis. 1966. "The Politics of the Mexican Labor Issue, 1950-1965." Agricultural History 157-176.

Hernandez, Daniel, Agustin Porras and Elena Zuniga. 1982. "Fertility Analysis in the Mexican Social Structure." In Jorge Martinez Manatou (ed.), The Demographic Revolution in Mexico 1970-1979. Mexico City: Mexican Institute of Social Security.

Hernandez, Jose, Leo Estrada, and David Alvirez. 1973. "Census Data and the Problem of Conceptually Defining the Mexican American Population." Social Science Quarterly 53(March): 671-687.

Hoffman, Abraham. 1974. Unwanted Americans in the Great Depression: Repatriation Pressures 1929-1939. Tucson: University of Arizona Press.

Hollerbach, Paula E. 1980. "Power in Families, Communication, and Fertility Decision-Making." Population and Environment 3:146-173.

Houstoun, Marion F. 1983. "Aliens in Irregular Status in the U.S.: A Review of Their Numbers, Characteristics, and Role in the U.S. Labor Market." Presented at the 6th Seminar in Adaptation and Integration of Immigrants, April 11-15, 1985, Geneva.

Jaffe, A.J., Ruth M. Cullen, and Thomas D. Boswell. 1980. The Changing Demography of Spanish Americans. New York: Academic Press.

Janis, I.L. and L. Mann. 1977. Decision Making. New York: The Free Press.

Jerome, Harry. 1926. Migration and Business Cycles. National Bureau of Economic Research. New York: NBER.

173

Jones, Richard C. 1984. "Changing Patterns of Undocumented Mexican Migration to South Texas." Social Science Quarterly 65(June): 465-481.

Kahn, Joan R. 1988. "Immigrant Selectivity and Fertility Adaptation in the United States." Social Forces 67(1): 108-128.

Kane, Thomas T., Siva Sivasubramaniam, and John Stanback. 1988. "Husband-Wife Attitudes, Communication, Contraceptive Decision Making and Consistency of Reporting in Sri Lanka." Presented at the annual meeting of the Population Association of America, New Orleans, April 21-23.

Keely, Charles B. 1972. "Immigration Recommendations of the Commission on Population Growth and the American Future." International Migration Review 6(3): 290-294.

Lee, Everett S. 1966. "A Theory of Migration." Demography 3(1): 47-56.

Lesko Associates. 1975. Basic Data and Guidance Required to Implement a Major Illegal Alien Study During Fiscal Year 1976. Final Report for Office of Planning and Evaluation, U.S. Immigration and Naturalization Service, Washington, D.C.

McConnell, Scott. 1988. "The New Battle over Immigration." Fortune 117(10): 89-102.

McLemore, S. Dale. 1983. Racial and Ethnic Relations in America, Second Edition. Boston: Allyn and Bacon, Inc.

174

McLemore, S. Dale and Ricardo Romo. 1985. "The Origins and Development of the Mexican American Ethnic Group." In R. de la Garza, F. Bean, C. Bonjean, R. Romo and R. Alvarez (eds.), The Mexican Origin Experience in the United States: An Interdisciplinary Anthology. Austin: The University of Texas Press.

McWilliams, Carey. 1968. North from Mexico: The Spanish-speaking People of the United States, Second Edition. New York: J.B. Lippincott Co.

Maram, Sheldon and Stewart Long. 1981. "The Labor-Market Impact of Hispanic Undocumented Workers: An Exploratory Study of the Garment Industry in Los Angeles County." California State University, Fullerton.

Mare, Robert D. 1981. "Change and Stability in Educational Stratification." American Sociological Review 46(February): 72-87.

Massey, Douglas S. 1981. "Dimensions of the New Immigration to the United States and Prospects for Assimilation." American Review of Sociology 7: 57-85.

_____. 1983. "A Research Note on Residential Succession: The Hispanic Case." Social Forces 61(March): 825-833.

Massey, Douglas S. and Brendan P. Mullan. 1984a. "Processes of Hispanic and Black Spatial Assimilation." American Journal of Sociology 89(January): 836-873.

_____. 1984b. "A Demonstration of the Effect of Seasonal Migration on Fertility." Demography 21(4): 501-518.

Mexico Instituto Nacional de Estadistica
Geografia e Informatica. 1983. X Censo General
de Poblacion y Vivienda: 1980. Resultados
Preliminares a Nivel Nacional y por Entidata
Federtiva. Mexico City.

Miller, Jerry L.L. and Maynard L. Erickson.
1981. "On Dummy Variable Regression Analysis:
A Description and Illustration of the Method."
In Peter V. Marsden (ed.), Linear Models in
Social Research. Beverly Hills: Sage
Publications.

Mines, Richard and Carole Frank Nuckton. 1982.
"The Evolution of Mexican Migration to the
United States: A Case Study." Giannini
Foundation Information Series 82-1, Division of
Agricultural Sciences, University of California.

Mirowsky, John and Catherine E. Ross. 1984.
"Language Networks and Social Status among
Mexican Americans." Social Science Quarterly
65(2): 551-564.

Montwieler, Nancy Humel. 1987. The Immigration
Reform Law of 1986: Analysis, Text and
Legislative History. Washington, D.C.: The
Bureau of National Affairs, Inc.

Moore, Joan W. 1970. Mexican Americans.
Englewood Cliffs, New Jersey: Prentice-Hall,
Inc.

Murguia, Edward. 1975. Assimilation,
Colonialism and the Mexican American People.
Austin: Center for Mexican American Studies,
The University of Texas at Austin.

Murguia, Edward and W. Parker Frisbie. 1977.
"Trends in Mexican American Intermarriage:
Recent Findings in Perspective," Social Science
Quarterly 58 (December): 374-389.

National Center for Health Statistics. 1985.
<u>Vital Statistics of the United States: 1980.</u>
<u>Mortality, Volume II, Part A.</u> Hyattsville, MD:
National Center for Health Statistics.

Neidert, Lisa J. and Reynolds Farley. 1985.
"Assimilation in the United States: An Analysis
of Ethnic and Generation Differences in Status
and Achievement." <u>American Sociological Review</u>
50(6): 840-850.

North, David S. and Marion F. Houstoun. 1976.
<u>The Characteristics and Role of Illegal Aliens</u>
<u>in the U.S. Labor Market: An Exploratory Study.</u>
Prepared for the Employment and Training
Administration, U.S. Department of Labor.

Opitz, Wolfgang and Parker Frisbie. 1985.
"Inconsistency in 1980 Marital Status Data:
Possible Solutions." Unpublished paper.

Ordorica, Manuel. 1984. "La Fecundidad en
Mexico 1940-1977." In Rene Jimenez Ornelas and
Alberto Minujin Zmud (eds.), <u>Los Factores del</u>
<u>Cambio Demografico en Mexico.</u> Mexico, D.F.:
Siglo Vienticinco Editores.

Ordorica, Manuel and Joseph Potter. 1981.
<u>Evaluation of the Mexican Fertility Survey 1976-</u>
<u>77. Scientific Reports No. 21.</u> London: World
Fertility Survey.

Park, Robert Ezra. 1950. <u>Race and Culture.</u>
Glencoe, IL: The Free Press.

Park, Robert Ezra and Ernest W. Burgess. 1969.
<u>Introduction to the Science of Sociology.</u>
Chicago: University of Chicago Press.

Pitt, Leonard. 1966. <u>The Decline of the</u>
<u>Californios: A Social History of the Spanish-</u>
<u>speaking Californians, 1946-1890.</u> Los Angeles:
University of California Press.

Plan Global de Desarrollo. 1980. S.P.P.
Mexico.

Portes, Alejandro. 1979. "Illegal Immigration
to the United States." Social Problems 26(4):
428-429.

_____. 1983. "International Labor Migration
and National Development." In Mary M. Kritz
(ed.), U.S. Immigration and Refugee Policy:
Global and Domestic Issues. Lexington, MA:
Lexington Books.

Portes, Alejandro and Robert L. Bach. 1985.
Latin Journey: Cuban and Mexican Immigrants in
the United States. Berkeley: University of
California Press.

Potter, Joseph E. 1983. "Effects of Societal
and Community Institutions on Fertility." In
Rodolfo A. Bulatao and Ronald D. Lee (eds.),
Determinants of Fertility in Developing
Countries. New York: Academic Press.

Pullum, Thomas W. 1980. "Separating Age,
Period, and Cohort Effects in White U.S.
Fertility, 1920-1970." Social Science Research
9: 225-244.

Pullum, Thomas W., John B. Casterline, and
Fatima Juarez. 1985. "Recent Trends in
Fertility and the Proximate Determinants in
Mexico." Presented at the Annual Meeting of the
Population Association of America, Boston, March
28-30.

Reichert, Josh and Douglas S. Massey. 1979.
"Patterns of U.S. Migration from a Mexican
Sending Community: A Comparison of Legal and
Illegal Immigrants." International Migration
Review 13(Winter): 599-623,

_____. 1980. "History and Trends in U.S.-Bound Migration from a Mexican Town. International Migration Review 14(Winter): 475-492.

Reisler, Mark. 1976. By the Sweat of Their Brow: Mexican Immigrant Labor in the United States, 1900-1940. Westport, CT: Greenwood.

Rindfuss, Ronald R. 1976. "Fertility and Migration: The Case of Puerto Rico." International Migration Review 10(2): 191-203.

Rindfuss, Ronald R. and James A. Sweet. 1977. Postwar Fertility Trends and Differentials in the United States. New York: Academic Press.

Rodriguez-Barocio, Raul, Jose Garcia-Nunez, Manuel Urban-Fuentes, and Deirdre Wulf. 1980. "Fertility and Family Planning in Mexico." International Family Planning Perspectives 6(1): 2-9.

Rosenwaike, Ira. 1973. "Two Generations of Italians in America: Their Fertility Experience." International Migration Review 7: 271-280.

Schedlin, Michele G. and Paula E. Hollerbach. 1981. "Modern and Traditional Fertility Regulation in a Mexican Community: The Process of Decision Making." Studies in Family Planning 12(6-7): 278-296.

Seiver, Daniel A. 1975. "Recent Fertility in Mexico: Measurement and Interpretation." Population Studies 29(3): 341-354.

Shapiro, Joseph P. 1988. "Getting in Before the Gate is Locked." U.S. News and World Report 104(18): 23-25.

Shaw, R. Paul. 1975. <u>Migration Theory and Fact.</u> Philadelphia: Regional Science Research Institute.

Shryock, Henry S., Jr. 1964. <u>Population Mobility Within the United States.</u> Chicago: Community and Family Study Center, University of Chicago.

Siegel, Jacob S., Jeffrey S. Passel, and J. Gregory Robinson. 1980. "Preliminary Review of Existing Studies of the Number of Illegal Residents in the United States." In <u>U.S. Immigration Policy and the National Interest,</u> the staff report of the Select Commission on Immigration and Refugee Policy, Appendix E: Papers on Illegal Immigration to the United States.

Singer, Audrey. 1988. "IRCA Aftermath." <u>Population Today</u> 16(10): 5, 9.

Smith-Lovin, Lynn and Ann R. Tickamyer. 1978. "Nonrecursive Models of Labor Force Participation, Fertility Behavior, and Sex Role Attitudes." <u>American Sociological Review</u> 43: 541-557.

St. John, Craig and Harold Grasmick. 1985. "Decomposing the Black/White Fertility Differential." <u>Social Science Quarterly</u> 66(1): 132-146.

Swicegood, Gray, Frank D. Bean, Elizabeth Hervey Stephen, and Wolfgang Opitz. 1988. "Language Usage and Fertility in the Mexican-Origin Population of the United States." <u>Demography</u> 25(1): 17-33.

Thomas, Dorothy S. 1938. <u>Research Memorandum on Migration Differentials.</u> New York: Social Science Research Council.

_____. 1941. <u>Social and Economic Aspects of Swedish Population Movements, 1750-1933.</u> New York: Macmillan Company.

Thomas, E. 1983. "Playing Politics with Immigration." <u>Time</u> 122 (October 17): 19.

Tienda, Marta. 1980. "Familism and Structural Assimilation of Mexican Immigrants in the United States." <u>International Migration Review</u> 14(3): 383-408.

_____. 1981. <u>Hispanic Origin Workers in the U.S. Labor Market.</u> Final Report to the U.S. Department of Labor, October.

Uhlenberg, Peter. 1973. "Fertility Patterns Within the Mexican-American Population." <u>Social Biology</u> 20(1): 30-39.

United Nations. 1975. <u>Demographic Yearbook: 1974.</u> New York: United Nations.

_____. 1986. <u>Demographic Yearbook: 1984.</u> New York: United Nations.

_____. 1988. <u>Demographic Yearbook: 1986.</u> New York: United Nations.

U.S. Bureau of the Census. 1960. <u>The Statistical History of the United States from Colonial Times to the Present.</u> Stamford, CT: Fairfield Publishers, Inc.

_____. 1982. <u>1980 Census of Population and Housing, Persons of Spanish Origin by State, Supplementary Report PC80-S1-7.</u> Washington, D.C.: Government Printing Office.

_____. 1983a. <u>1980 Census of Population and Housing, General Population Characteristics United States Summary PC80-1-B1.</u> Washington D.C.: Government Printing Office.

_____. 1983b. <u>1980 Census of Population and Housing, General Social and Economic Characteristics, United States Summary PC80-1-C1.</u> Washington, D.C.: Government Printing Office.

_____. 1983c. <u>1980 Census of Population and Housing: Public-Use Microdata Samples. Technical Documentation.</u> Washington, D.C.: Data Users Service Division, Bureau of the Census.

U.S. Department of Justice. 1981. <u>1981 Statistical Yearbook of the Immigration and Naturalization Service.</u> Washington, D.C.: Government Printing Office.

_____. 1988. <u>1987 Statistical Yearbook of the Immigration and Naturalization Service.</u> Washington, D.C.: Government Printing Office.

<u>U.S. News and World Report.</u> 1982. "Gate Starts Closing on Illegal Aliens." 92(August 30): 8.

Van Arsodol, M.D., Jr., G.Z. Sabagh, and E.W. Butler. 1968. "Retrospective and Subsequent Residential Mobility." <u>Demography</u> 5: 249-267.

Ventura, Stephanie J. 1983. "Births of Hispanic Parentage." National Center for Health Statistics <u>Monthly Vital Health Statistics Reports</u> 31(6S). Hyattsville, MD: Public Health Service.

Waldinger, Roger. 1984. "The Occupational And Economic Integration of the New Immigrants." In Richard R. Hofstetter (ed.), <u>U.S. Immigration Policy.</u> Durham: Duke University Press.

Warren, Robert and Jeffrey S. Passel. 1987. "A Count of the Uncountable: Estimates of Undocumented Aliens Counted in the 1980 Census." <u>Demography</u> 24(3): 375-393.

Warner, W. Lloyd and Leo Srole. 1945. The Social Systems of American Ethnic Groups. New Haven: Yale University Press.

Warwick, Donald P. 1982. Bitter Pills: Population Policies and their Implementation in Eight Developing Countries. Cambridge: Cambridge University Press.

Weber, David J. 1973. Foreigners in their Native Land. Albuquerque: University of New Mexico Press.

Weber, David J. 1982. The Mexican Frontier, 1821-1846: The American Southwest Under Mexico. Albuquerque: University of New Mexico Press.

Welch, Susan and John R. Hibbing. 1984. "Hispanic Representation in the U.S. Congress." Social Science Quarterly 65(2): 328-335.

Westinghouse Health Systems. 1978. Mexico Contraceptive Prevalence Survey Summary Report. Columbia, Maryland: Westinghouse Health Systems.

Westoff, Charles F. and Norman B. Ryder. 1977. The Contraceptive Revolution. Princeton: Princeton University Press.

World Fertility Survey. 1980. The Mexico Fertility Survey, 1976-1977: A Summary of Findings. Number 17. London: World Fertility Survey.

World Fertility Survey. 1981. Mexico Fertility Survey Codebook. WFS/Tech. 1654. London: World Fertility Survey.

Zazueta, Carlos H. and Rodolfo Corona. 1979.
"Los Trabajadores Mexicanos en los Estados
Unidos: Primeros Resultados de la Encuesta
Nacional de Emigracion." Mexico City: Centro
Nacional de Informacion y Estadisticas del
Trabajo.